Rave Reviews f  ok

"Some say the practice of law is an art but it is rare to find a resource that thoroughly addresses this aspect of training to be a lawyer. *The Happy Law Practice* does just that and more. Being proficient in the law is sometimes not enough but this book addresses managing priorities, networking for results, and building your brand. Beyond these macro skills, it provides a guide on how to deal with the details of day-to-day practice including well being, often overlooked in maintaining health and good business." -*Anne Gwal, Associate General Counsel to a Fortune 500 Company and President of a local Affinity Bar Association*

"*The Happy Law Practice* is a MUST read for anyone who has, or plans to have, an Esq. at the end of his/her name. The changes in law firms over the decades have really required a how-to-guide for lawyers of all ages; *The Happy Law Practice* fits the bill perfectly. It is not only a guide to running a successful law practice but also to living a healthy life as a lawyer. It is possible to be a successful lawyer without billing 300 hours a month! This book provides the necessary tools for lawyers of all ages. Thank you for this book!" -*Genavieve Shingle, Genavieve Shingle Law (genavieveshingle.com)*

"Inspiring and energizing: a must read for every lawyer, with excellent tips and wise advice to boost personal development while striking the right balance." -*Pascale De Jonckheere, Founder and Director, Three Points Legal Solutions – Corporate legal consultancy and interim management, Brussels (threepoints.eu)*

The Happy Law Practice

*Expert Strategies to Build Business
While Maintaining Peace of Mind*

ESQUIRE COACHING

Leading Attorneys to Extraordinary Personal & Professional Success

About Esquire Coaching

Esquire Coaching is exclusively committed to the professional and personal success of lawyers. It's not enough to be a brilliant attorney to succeed in today's economic environment.

We teach our clients how to be strategic and equip them with the right skills in business development, to help them succeed.

With our broad array of consultants, ranging from business coaches to image consultants (and everything in between!), we are a one-stop shop to help attorneys acquire the skills they need to have extraordinary personal and professional success.

We will teach you how to be a rainmaker achieve work-life balance gain job satisfaction or get a new job be a leader improve your personal brand & image

Want expert tips and resources for attorney success delivered to your doorstep? Visit www.EsquireCoaching.com to sign up for Elevate! — Esquire's newsletter, including exclusive offers.

The Happy Law Practice

*Expert Strategies to Build Business
While Maintaining Peace of Mind*

Co-authored by

Gila Lee Adato   José Albino   Nancy Barrood
Nilda Carrasquillo   Tracy Dacko   Mary E. Davis
Margo DeGange   Jean Hanham   Mirna Hidalgo
Ann Jenrette-Thomas   Nicole K. Lundy   Jill Magerman
Ketema Mason   Amy Neiman   Sandra Olper
Vikram Rajan   Jennifer Robinson   Jason Rodriguez
Fred Schuldt   Donna Spina   Melody Stevens

Compiled by

Ann Jenrette-Thomas, Esq.

Splendor Publishing
College Station, TX.

SPLENDOR PUBLISHING
Published by Splendor Publishing
College Station, TX.

First published printing, March 2014

Library of Congress Control Number: 2014931620
The Happy Law Practice
Expert Strategies to Build Business While Maintaining Peace of Mind
1. Law
2. Business

ISBN-10:1940278066
ISBN-13:978-1-940278-06-3

Printed in the United States of America.

Cover Image: YuliaGlam 819701 | Vectorstock

For more information, or to order bulk copies of this book, please
contact the author.

Dedication

This book is dedicated to all of the lawyers who entered
the law believing that they could make a positive difference
while having a good life, but subsequently lost hope that
they could have it all. May this book help restore your faith
and give you back a life that you deserve.

.

Contents

Part III
Special Strategies for Law Firm Partners

Part IV
Cultivating Peace of Mind

Introduction

by Ann Jenrette-Thomas, Esq., CPCC,
CEO of Esquire Coaching

A Happy Law Practice? Yeah right! Whether you're a solo/small firm partner or a law firm Associate who wants to make partner, the idea of happily and successfully building your legal practice while maintaining peace of mind seems like an impossibility.

Practicing law in and of itself is stressful. It requires us to work grueling hours, stay on top of the latest developments in our practice area, and meet the demands and pressures of effectively representing our clients. Oftentimes, we barely feel like we can keep our head above water! In fact, a recent survey conducted by Esquire Coaching revealed that the number one complaint among the lawyers surveyed is lack of work-life balance.

In this day and age, being a phenomenal lawyer isn't enough. If you want to have a thriving legal career, you have to learn how to think like a successful entrepreneur, regardless of whether you are a sole proprietor, a partner in a small firm, or a law firm Associate. Why should we think like successful entrepreneurs? Successful entrepreneurs realize that:

- Their *first* responsibility is to build their client or customer base, regardless of their trade or craft, because their livelihood depends on it.

- Their business should support and work around the lifestyle they want to live (not the other way around).

- If they don't balance their life and take care of themselves, they can't be their best, which in turn impacts their bottom line and the quality of their services.

Won't thinking like a successful entrepreneur make my life harder? Not only do I have to still be a great lawyer, now I'm supposed to build business skills too?

The truth is, while it may take some time to master the different skills necessary to build a successful business, these skills will make you indispensable. They ensure that you know how to develop your own book of business, while always keeping an eye toward managing the needs of your personal life.

For example, Associates who know how to bring in business are more valuable to the firm and thus become partner faster than those who don't. Similarly, as a law firm partner, knowing how to build business will ensure that you can stay in business longer and make more money to support the lifestyle you want to live.

Okay, I understand why it is important to think like a successful entrepreneur, but how will this make me happy?

As noted above, successful entrepreneurs know how to make their businesses work around their personal lives. They are intentional about ensuring that they can have the money and time they need to enjoy life and their loved ones. More importantly, they make self-care a priority, recognizing that if they do not tend to their physical, emotional, spiritual, and financial needs, they just won't have the bandwidth to properly take care of their clients/customers, much less build a sustainable business.

Introduction

How can this book help me?

In creating this book, I reached out to a number of successful lawyers and entrepreneurs to write a chapter in which they share some of their best tips and insights as it pertains to their particular area of expertise. To this end, this book is divided into four parts:

Part 1: Look and Act Like a Rainmaker

This section consists of six chapters that teach you a variety of skills to help you "make rain" (i.e., build business through a solid and loyal client base). Chapter 1 provides a foundation from which you can better understand your purpose and the legacy you want to leave. In chapters 2 and 3, you'll learn how to get an edge over your competition by developing a personal brand and how to look the part of a successful lawyer. Chapters 4-6 walk you through concrete marketing and sales skills that will help your ideal prospective clients know about your services, begin to trust your expertise, and hire you (preferably again and again!).

Being a successful rainmaker is an art. By practicing the information in each of these chapters, you are well on your way to becoming an indispensable rainmaker.

Part 2: Stand Out from the Crowd—Be a Better and More Productive Lawyer

This section consists of five chapters that will help you stand out from the sea of lawyers. There are over 1.2 million lawyers in the United States alone. In order to stand out from the crowd, you have to think and act differently than most lawyers. Chapters 7-9 offer different strategies to approach your legal practice and the way that you interact with clients. Chapters 10-11 offer practical tips and insights to increase your productivity by improving both your organizational and time management skills.

Part 3: Special Strategies for Law Firm Partners

This section consists of four chapters specifically designed to assist law firm partners, especially those of solo or small firms. Chapter 12 offers concrete tips on how to adopt a mindset that will allow you to succeed as you face the challenges of building a solo (or small firm) practice. Chapter 13 provides the new business owner concrete tips to understand and stay on top of the basics of small business finance. To help ease the challenges of developing and growing your business, chapters 14 and 15 teach you how to hire your dream team and celebrate them so they continue to produce the best results for your firm.

Part 4: Cultivating Peace of Mind

This section consists of six chapters that will help you cultivate peace of mind and achieve greater work-life balance. In chapters 16-18, you will learn the different types of stress and concrete strategies to manage negative stress, and take care of yourself and your key relationships. Chapters 19-20 help you to cultivate inner peace through strategies to honor your spirit and your energy levels. In our final chapter (Chapter 21), you will learn to define (or redefine) success in a way that authentically honors who you are.

Some of the concepts in this book may be new to you. Keep an open mind as you read. Use the tips and strategies that work for you and leave the rest. Each chapter stands alone, so feel free to read the chapters in any order you like or skip those chapters that do not apply or appeal to you.

Introduction

Our intention in creating this book is to have experts in a variety of fields offer you concrete, actionable tips and strategies that will live up to the title of this book—teaching you to create a happy law practice while maintaining peace of mind.

We'd love to hear from you! Tell us which strategies worked for you and which didn't. Tell us your war stories and your triumphs. You can e-mail us at **info@EsquireCoaching.com.** Of course, if you need additional support on your journey to achieving a happy law practice while maintaining peace of mind, reach out to the team at **EsquireCoaching.com** or any of the individual authors directly (see their chapters for each author's contact information).

Here's to *your* happy law practice!

Part I

Look and Act Like a Rainmaker

Chapter 1
Live Your Intended Legacy
by Jean Hanham

What are you most passionate about? What do you love to do? When are you happiest? What makes you come alive? What do you want to be remembered for? Are you living your intended legacy?

These powerful questions are often placed on the sidelines of life because our busy schedules get in the way. We move through the days, weeks, months, and years at lightening speed to get it all done. Appointments, meetings, events, court dates, office work, deadlines, and general daily commitments all seem so important. We forget to consider that we'll wake up one morning wondering where the years have gone and if we've done something with our life that really mattered and for which we will be remembered. We'll find ourselves reflecting on the choices we've made and evaluating whether or not we've taken time to enjoy meaningful moments along the way. It's typically then, when it feels too late, that these questions place themselves front-and-center and we wish we'd taken some time to consider them earlier in life.

Unfortunately, the truth is, too often we live our lives making decisions based on what we think we should do or based on what we feel others expect of us, rather than centered on what we truly value and want. We ignore what is most important to us and we follow the footsteps created by someone else, rather than creating our own path. We may choose to avoid the pain, discomfort, and disappointments that we fear will accompany our journey if we dream too big and go for what we really want. We may simply decide to settle for "good enough." As a result, the true leader within us sleeps, the impact we have is marginalized, and we don't live up to our fullest potential.

In the article, "Regrets of the Dying," palliative care nurse, Bronnie Ware, shares regrets she heard from her patients during their last three to twelve weeks of life. The most common regret noted was, "I wish I'd had more courage to live a life true to myself, not the life that others expected of me."

Consider for just a moment if you are really living life true to yourself. If you are, BRAVO! Stay the course. You are creating your intended legacy! If you are not, isn't it time to ask, "Why not?" More importantly, isn't it time to do something about it?

Choosing to live your intended legacy is a journey that begins with self-awareness. You have to know what it is you want because your legacy is all about you: the person you are when no one is looking, the person you are at home, at work, in your community, and beyond. It is about your values, your goals, your passions and your dreams. It is about what is most fulfilling to you as a human being, and about the steps you've taken to move in that direction with accountability for the choices you've made each day. It is about achieving success as *you* chose to define it. It is about how you've creatively blended your strengths, values, and aspirations to intentionally create the life that you want to live.

Those who embark on the journey dare to know themselves and what they want. They are willing to face their fears, and are willing to get uncomfortable for the sake of moving in the direction they want to go. They are individuals who know they want to live their life with passion and purpose, and who will do what it takes to accomplish just that. It's hard work, it takes courage, it's worth it, and you can do it if you choose.

As a lawyer, you know about hard work. You've had to put forth great effort to reach the levels of intellect and technical excellence that are critically important for success in your profession. From experience, you know and can appreciate that it takes focus, effort and persistence to overcome challenges and obstacles that stand between you and your goals. You recognize that when you commit and apply yourself, anything is possible. If you are ready to bring that same energy and effort to living your intended legacy, you can create what you want in your life, and the most common regret of the dying will not be one that you share.

Get Ready, Set, Go!

Yes, the assumption is here that you are choosing to embark on the journey. To help you get started, following are a series of thought-provoking exercises designed for you to learn more about yourself. Complete them in order, and take your time. Know that the work you do here may result in a desire for adjustments or minor tweaks to life, as you know it. It may awaken a hunger for major changes; perhaps even an over-haul. Or, it may simply serve as confirmation that you are actually right where you want to be. Just try to remain curious about what you learn as you go, and trust in the process. Living your intended legacy is a life-long endeavor; this is just the beginning.

Before you jump in, make one commitment. Promise to always appreciate yourself for where you are right here in this current moment. Don't be a self-critic, and no judging please. We are not in a courtroom! Trust that wherever you are is exactly where you are meant to be. What you learn about yourself and the choices you make going forward are all that matter.

Plan to complete each exercise in a place that is comfortable and where you will be free of distractions and interruptions. Also, have paper and a pen handy. Often, you will be asked to answer questions, reflect, and take notes on your experiences.

Exercise 1: Who Am I?

Get naked! Not literally, just figuratively! This is an exercise to get in touch with the real you. Remove the armor you wear. This includes your GPA, the schools you've attended, degrees and titles you hold, firms that you've worked for, your accomplishments, the money you've made, and the possessions you own. It also includes throwing away how others have defined you. Be willing to stand just as you are without all that "stuff."

Consider this question: who am I?

Notice what you notice. Be willing to be vulnerable and simply connect with who you really are and what you feel. These moments of being alone with ourselves are often few and far between, yet they hold so much information for us.

Consider this question (again): who am I?

Write down your answers as well as the feeling that emerged during this exercise.

Exercise 2: Wake Up Your Leader

We all have a leader within us. Our leader is our unique inner voice that reminds us to dream big, feel deeply, learn, grow, take action, and become all that we are meant to be in the world. When we nurture and care for the leader within us, we increase our self-awareness and we are more likely to consciously make choices that are in alignment with our goals and our dreams. When we increase our self-awareness, we cannot ignore this inner voice, it speaks too loudly.

This exercise is meant to help you reconnect with the passion, creativity, and inspiration that reside within you. Take a bit of time to consider the following powerful questions:

• What am I most passionate about?

- What do I love to do?

- When am I happiest?

- What makes me come alive?

- What do I want to be remembered for?

- What is most important to me?

- What do I most value?

- Am I living my intended legacy?

- How do I know?

You may find these questions easy to answer, or you may find them to be challenging. Give yourself permission to take the time needed to come up with thoughtful, honest, and heartfelt answers. Don't overthink your answers. Trust your gut. There is no right or wrong answer. Write down your answers.

Deepen what you learn by sharing your answers in conversation with a close friend whom you trust will not judge you—someone who will support you and your dreams. Notice what you notice.

Here are a few additional questions to consider:

- What am I learning about myself?

- Am honoring those things that are most important to me in the decisions and choices that I make each day?

- What is alive inside me as I answer these questions?

Write down your answers.

Exercise 3: Where Am I Now? Where Do I Want To Be?

This is an assessment exercise. You are simply taking inventory of where you are right now and where you want to be. Ask yourself the following questions and write down your answers:

- Is my work fulfilling? Why or why not?

- What is missing?

- What would make my work a perfect "10"?

- If time and resources were not of concern, what do I enjoy doing in my free time?

- How often do I do those things I most enjoy?

- What are my priorities in life?

- What do I value most in life?

- What would make my life a perfect "10"?

- What do I want more of in my life?

- What do I want less of in my life?

- What am I tolerating in my life?

Based on your answers, consider where you are now and where you want to be. What is the distance and geography between the two points? You can write about it or draw a picture that captures your thoughts.

Exercise 4: Facing My Fears

To get from where you are today to where you want to be, you need to identify the challenges and obstacles that stand in the way.

What stands in your way? For some, it is an old story that we tell ourselves, or we feel we are victims of our circumstances (this is actually a version of an old story). For most, it's fear. It could be fear of failure, fear of being wrong, fear of rejection, fear of being emotionally uncomfortable, fear of not being liked, fear of being seen as weak, fear of letting someone down, fear of not being good enough, and the list goes on.

Be honest with yourself, what is really standing in the way of getting to where you want to be?

Recognize that we all have fears and challenges to overcome. It is part of being human. The question is whether you will let those challenges and fears get in your way. Will you allow them to hold you back from living your intended legacy?

Consider this: what is one thing you can do today that will help you to overcome the challenges or fears that stand in your way?

Exercise 5: Letter to Self

This is an annual exercise to set intentions for creating and living the life that you dream of.

Begin right now by writing a letter to yourself dated one year from today. This is a letter written to you by yourself.

The letter is an opportunity to share all of the amazing things that you've accomplished next year "as if" they have already happened. This is the key, "as if" they have already happened. This letter should be crafted in alignment with living your legacy.

Include what you are most proud of, what challenges you have overcome, and what you are most excited about as you continue on your journey. Do not make the letter about what others have done or have not done; instead keep it focused on you and what you can control. Once written, put it in an envelope, seal it up, and place it somewhere for safe keeping until this time next year.

The impact of this exercise can be life changing. When you are clear on who you are, what's important to you, where you want to be, and what things you want to prioritize, your life more easily changes to match those desires! Much like the *Law of Attraction*, if you believe it, feel it, and embody it, it will become you!

Exercise 6: My Plan of Action

You are at a decision point. It is time to move from intention setting to creating a plan of action to achieve what you want. Those who write down their goals and their plan of action have the highest probability for success. Are you really committed? Are you ready to make a plan and to hold yourself accountable for living your intended legacy?

Begin by defining your WHY? Why is it important to you that you accomplish what you've set out to do in your life? When you know your personal why, you are much more likely to take action.

Next, create and commit to a plan that brings you to where you want to be. What can you do today to bring you one step closer to where you want to be in your life? SMART goals work best, as they are *Specific, Measurable, Attainable, Relevant* and *Time-Bound.*

Then, take action and follow through on it. Make a point to do something each and every day that is aligned with the life you want to live.

Lastly, define how you will hold yourself accountable. What can you put in place that will help to ensure that you stay true to yourself and what you want to achieve?

You might consider working with an accountability partner or hiring a professional coach. These are valuable resources to help you keep on track.

Congratulations! If you have taken the time to read through this chapter, and to complete all of the exercises, you are one step closer today to living your intended legacy. Stay focused and committed . . . you are worth it.

Remember always that how you live your life is a choice. It is *your* life and *your* choice. Choose consciously, choose honestly, and choose wisely; choose to live *your* intended legacy!

"Don't ask what the world needs. Ask what makes you come alive, and go do it. Because what the world needs is people who have come alive." —Howard Thurman

About Jean Hanham

As a certified coach, creative workshop designer, skilled facilitator & inspiring speaker, Jean's success is fueled by her passion for living life to its fullest and her unique ability enabling others to do the same! Jean spent 20 years in leadership roles at Catalina Marketing, Imagitas and Affinnova. She holds her BA from Rutgers University, MBA from Columbia University and she's a graduate of CRR and CTI's global coaching certification programs. Jean is part of the Esquire Coaching team.

Website: atriolifecoaches.com
Facebook: facebook.com/jean.hanham
LinkedIn: linkedin.com/in/jeanhanham

Chapter 2
The Laws of Personal Branding
for Leading-Edge Lawyers
by Nicole K. Lundy

Y̶ou are one in over a million—literally.

The American Bar Association has reported that in 2013, there were 1.3 million licensed lawyers just in the United States alone. That means if you are a lawyer right now or in pursuit of a law career, you have to make a critical choice if you want to have a dynamic legal career and be a leading-edge lawyer.

The critical choice is this: you must create an intentional game plan using **The 5 Essential Elements of Personal Branding**. They are:

1. Alignment—getting clear on your real personal brand as a leading-edge lawyer

2. Influence—presenting your authority as a leading-edge lawyer

3. Command—designing a wardrobe that makes you look like a leading-edge lawyer

4. Visibility—creating a plan to get out there in a BIG way

5. Conversion—having more captivating conversations with prospects that will make them all say "Yes" to working with you

Here's what I've discovered to be true. Gone are the days of just passing the bar, renting an office space or getting hired by a prestigious law firm, working thousands of grueling hours per year, getting business cards with your "First Name, Last Name, Esq." printed on heavy cardstock paper, and buying a closet full of black, blue and grey suits in the name of being a leading lawyer. This alone is not enough to earn your credibility stripes. There are a million (literally) others working this same plan.

It's also the formula for having a bland legal career. You know, the kind of career that motivates you to poke a pencil in your right eyeball for fun every day? Yes, that type of bland.

We are now in the era of Human Business. No longer does being a lawyer imply that you work only behind the scenes. Being a lawyer *now* means that your personal brand and legal career go hand-in-hand. No longer can you hide behind your law school's reputation, your firm's logo or in that suit. It just won't work.

You are the living, breathing, and walking representation of how dynamic your legal career really is. It's a huge deal and even bigger responsibility. So let's start with **alignment**—getting clear on your real personal brand as a leading-edge lawyer.

The entire point of personal branding is for people to *know-like-trust* you. The "people" that I am referring to are your prospects, clients, and peers.

Let's face it, lawyers have a bad reputation. We don't have to get into the specifics of the reputation, but generally lawyers are not considered too trustworthy.

When others *know-like-trust* you as a lawyer, you will immediately stand out as a leading-edge lawyer with priceless career benefits that include credibility, authenticity, great reputation, trustworthiness, and undeniable expertise.

Let's dig a little deeper. Before anybody can *know-like-trust* you as a lawyer, you must have a "Personal Brand."

So, now the million-dollar question is, what is *your* personal brand? Can you answer that *now*? My guess is that your mind just went blank.

The definition that I have coined that answers this question is: *it's your exclusive guarantee of market value.* It's what you do and how you do it, in your own special way.

Let's take a look at one of the greatest Personal Brand icons in my humble opinion—Oprah Winfrey. Oprah's exclusive guarantee of market value is *empathy.* (She has others but empathy is definitely in her top three.) Empathy is in every single thing that she does and delivers—it's in her tone of voice, body language, words, how she tells a story—just about *everything*! It's part of her Personal Brand DNA and she is in complete *alignment* with it. Oprah is magnetic because of her alignment, and her success as a businesswoman is also attributed to her being aligned with her Personal Brand.

To get in alignment with your Personal Brand and be a leading-edge lawyer, you must know your value proposition, what makes you different, and your marketability.

Answer these three questions in detail:

1. Value Proposition: what do you stand for?

2. Differentiation: what makes you stand out?

3. Marketability: what makes you compelling?

Now, let's talk **influence**—presenting your authority as a leading-edge lawyer. Having influence as a lawyer is crucial to your career longevity and trajectory. Most importantly, it's critical to you being a leading-edge lawyer.

The key to creating influence in your legal career is *mastering your target market* using your **value**, **story** and **leadership**.

Value: your value as a lawyer is the legal solutions you provide that makes your client's life better. Also, you:

- Keep your promises and maintain a high standard of the services and products that your target market knows to expect.

- Are consistent with the message of who you are and what you stand for.

Story: your *Brand Story* is the story that portrays the heart and soul of your legal career and emotionally connects your brand with your clients. You use your Brand Story to communicate what you stand for, what you promise, and what your client's experience.

There are seven story types. Which one is *your* Personal Brand as a lawyer, telling?

1. Overcoming the Monster—classic underdog story

2. Rebirth—story of renewal

3. Quest—a mission from point A to point B

4. Journey & Return—transformation through travel and homecoming

5. Rags to Riches—rising from the ashes

6. Tragedy—the dark side of humanity and the future nature of human experience

7. Comedy—the flipside of tragedy

How do you craft your Brand Story? Here are a series of questions to answer that are all a part of your Brand Story. When you have finished answering all of the questions, you will put the story together:

1. What do you do?

2. What are you attracted to (concepts, things, people)?

3. What do people praise you for the most?

4. Now, think about your business (career, vocation). How has your relationship to what you do changed over time? What did you learn on your way to where you are now? How did you affect others by what you do?

5. Why do you do what you do?

6. What are you passionate about the most in your business? What makes you feel alive?

7. What are your goals for the future?

8. What are your favorite colors, foods, books, movies, objects, places (anything favorite that comes to mind)?

9. Do you have any personal quirks?

10. What are three words that describe you?

Now, review your answers and see which of the aforementioned seven story styles would best fit what you've written. Then, take some time to truly craft your Brand Story. The most important thing to remember about your Brand Story is that your story should support your core brand message.

Leadership: first things first—you need to get clear on your *Leadership Behavior Style.* Why? John C. Maxwell (acclaimed author) sums it up concisely—"Leadership is influence." If you are not perceived as a leader, you will have to convince every single prospect, client, and peer of your worth and credibility as a skilled and leading-edge lawyer.

Here's a list of the most common leadership styles. Pick up to three of the styles that resonate with you the most:

- Problem Solver

- Referee (settles interpersonal conflict)

- Process Manager (ensures that goals are met)

- Procurer (finds and manages resources)

- Visionary

- Crisis Manager (puts out everyday fires)

- Motivator

- Task Master

- Counselor (helps with personal issues)

- Risk Taker

- Expert

After you are clear on your Leadership Behavior Style, the next step is to get clear on your approach to leadership. What this means is "how do you like to lead?"

Here is a pretty extensive list for you to go through. Review thoroughly and see what resonates with you. Pick up to five words from the list and complete this sentence: "_____ is a cornerstone in my approach to leadership."

Achievement
Adventure
Challenge
Control
Creativity
Economic Balance
Fairness
Freedom
Happiness
Hard Work
Honesty
Harmony
Involvement
Order
Affection
Comfort
Conformity
Cooperation
Directness
Expertness
Flexibility

Friendship
Helpfulness
Independence
Integrity
Leadership
Morality/Ethics
Loyalty
Predictability
Responsibility
Responsiveness
Personal Development
Power
Recognition
Risk
Self-Respect
Variety
Security
Trust
Tradition
Wisdom

Next, let's discuss **command**—designing a wardrobe that makes you look like a leading-edge lawyer.

It's not enough to be great—you have to *look* great too. Whether you accept it or not, perception is what makes you fly or flop in your law career. In other words, you can be *the* smartest lawyer in the entire planet, but if you look sloppy, you won't be taken seriously, be seen as trust-worthy or considered a leader. Shallow? Maybe. However, this is how we humans work. We judge every single thing. Nowadays, you are judged on more than the law school you attended, your internship with the Supreme Court Judge, or the law firm where you toil away six and a half days every week. Simply put, this is just not enough to make you stand out from the pack. It's not enough to make you the crème de la crème of the legal industry.

The obvious question now, is 'well, how do I become seen as a valuable lawyer?' The easiest way I can answer this is 'define your personal brand.' The reason why, is that this is the only thing that nobody else can copy. You are the originator and the only version of you.

The foundation of your personal brand is your professional presentation. You must look like you are ready for the spotlight at any given moment. This means that you must find a grooming regimen that fits into your grueling schedule and a power wardrobe that gives you the appearance of looking smart and savvy. I know that you are busy paying your dues, and working tons of hours and playing your part to reach the top of the game. However, if you walk around your firm, meet clients and present yourself as if you are overworked, you set yourself back by at least one century. Here's why. No longer can you hide behind a prestigious law firm name or logo because, today, every lawyer represents himself or herself. You are solely responsible for being recognized as a leading-edge lawyer or not.

Lawyer-Friendly Grooming Regimen

Here are grooming and wardrobe tips that you can use today to improve your professional presentation so that you are always seen as polished and sharp.

It's very easy to look haggard and over-worked as a lawyer. There are not enough hours in the day for you to attend to your appearance. Here are three easy ways for you to look refreshed during the entire day:

- **Cleansing Wipes**—From now on, consider these to be apart of your career success team. Always keep them on hand, for you to maintain a fresh and clean appearance. Stress often causes the sebum production in your skin to go into over-drive, which results in you looking like last week—oily and yucky. The great part is that you can also replace the cleansing wipes with your regular cleanser at home to keep your skin regimen as simple as possible.

- **Whitening Strips**—Yes, it is true that a lot of lawyers drink a crap load of coffee, resulting in yellow-brownish teeth. This is not the look that you want. You don't have to lose your coffee habit (I know it's part of your survival!), but add whitening strips to your to-do list a few times a week, to keep your teeth looking nice. As a lawyer, you communicate a lot, and your teeth are hard to hide.

- **Lip Balm**—A lot of talking, long hours, and stress lead to chapped, dry lips. Now be honest with yourself, when you see somebody with chapped lips, do you focus on anything they are saying? Exactly. This also applies to you as a lawyer even though you are giving great advice at $300+ per billable hour. Lip balm is created in small convenient packaging, which makes it easy for you to discretely apply before an important client meeting, court appearance, or conference.

Power Wardrobe

Yes, it's true that being a lawyer is a road traveled only by exceptional people and ideally that should be enough to signify that you are a powerful lawyer. But, it's not. You must insinuate your power through your wardrobe on a regular basis. Here are three easy ways to do this:

• **Incorporate Dynamo Elements**—For men, this would be your power tie – red or blue. For women, this would be your power lipstick, blue-red for cool undertones and orange-red for warm undertones. Now, you don't have to overdue this and insert a dynamo element into your everyday working wardrobe. However, you must discern which events and meetings that you need to play your power card. This is when you step up and present yourself with either your power tie or lipstick.

• **Color Coordinates**—Typically, lawyers go out and fill their closets with black suits. The reality is that black does not look great on everybody's skin tone. In fact, wearing black can be the worst choice for some lawyers. Instead wearing blues and greys is the best option. Wearing the right color suit is very important. Here's a tip, if you have cool skin undertones, black suits will suit you and if you have warm skin undertones, blue suits look best. Grey colored suits look good on most skin tones.

• **Clean Shoes**—Not much else says unprofessional like dirty and scruffy shoes. Whether your shoes are off the runways of fashion week or from a discount retailer, they need to be intact at all times. This applies to men and women lawyers. Clean shoes gives you the appearance of being a professional, well-put together lawyer. Dirty and scruffy shoes say the opposite. (For more information on wardrobe, see Chapter 3.)

Finding a grooming routine and coordinating a power wardrobe that works for you are an essential part of becoming a leading-edge lawyer. Perception is everything in creating a thriving legal career.

It's time for **visibility**—creating a plan to get out there in a BIG way.

Building your platform is key to getting strategic visibility in your legal career. The higher the platform, the better for being a leading-edge lawyer.

Here are my top three strategies that I personally use with my private clients to create a high platform and get out there in a BIG way:

1. Social Influence—Nowadays, if you are not on social media in some capacity, you are invisible. Although 'time' is a huge factor as a lawyer because of all of the required hours, you only need to be on platforms where your clients are. Do some research and survey your current clients to find out where they are hanging out online. When you find out where they are, share valuable information with them on a consistent basis. There is a huge opportunity here for you, as lawyers are commonly deemed 'unapproachable'.

2. Speaking—Speaking is an incredible way to build your credibility. Create an uncanny 'signature talk' that ties your specialty in law to how it adds enormous value in other's lives. I guarantee you that this visibility strategy will set you apart right away. There are so many unanswered legal questions that the regular John and Jane Doe never get answered because the world of 'law' seems so foreign to them. Groups that typically need speakers and would love a unique take on talking about "law" include: chambers of commerce; business networking and professional groups; professional associations; trade groups; and charitable organizations.

3. Fame Name—Craft a "Fame Name" that highlights your unique specialty as a lawyer. It's your very own personal headline and describes yourself in a short and concise way. For example, can you be "Ali Smith, the Entrepreneur's Lawyer" OR "Ted Thompson, the First-Time Homebuyer's Lawyer." This is a game-changing strategy.

Lastly, let's talk **conversion**—having captivating conversations with prospects and clients that make them say "Yes" to working with you.

This is important. If nobody likes talking to you, then you won't be a lawyer for too long. Well, let me revise that statement. You won't be a leading-edge lawyer if nobody likes talking to you.

So, what's the strategy? Ease up on the legal lingo!

When people need a lawyer, their biggest concern is that the potential lawyer they are speaking to "gets" them. They can clearly see your law degree and other credentials hanging on the wall or on your website. You definitely don't need to prove yourself anymore by using legal lingo that flies over their head.

Use and follow this simple **5-step captivating conversation formula:**

1. Dream—Get an inspired vision on why they need legal help right now. **Ask them:**

-What do you need right now?
-What's the biggest problem you're facing right now?

2. Booby Trap—Find the block that has stopped them from getting legal help before. **Ask them:**

-Why don't you think you're getting that?
-What do you think has been holding you back?

3. Aftermath—Get them in touch with their pain and sense of urgency. **Ask them:**

-What happens if nothing changes and you don't get the legal help you need?
-What would potentially stop you?

4. Guide—Connect the dots for them and show them how you can help them (you must articulate it for them). **Ask them:**

-Based on what you said, the obstacle is [paraphrase obstacle]. If you were able to [identify steps they need to take to resolve their obstacle], would you agree that you could achieve your goal?
-Well, from what you told me, it sounds like you need [appropriate legal solutions you could provide to resolve obstacle] to move forward, would you agree?

5. Ask—Diagnose and prescribe the exact legal solution that would solve their problem. **Tell them:**

-Well, the great news is our [legal service] does all we talked about and will get you the [solution] you're looking for.

Your law career is depending on *you*! You now have the tools to craft a strategic Personal Brand Plan to stand out and step into the spotlight as a leading-edge lawyer.

About Nicole K. Lundy

Nicole K. Lundy, Speaker, Author and Profitable Personal Brand Strategist, helps high-achieving professionals be seen as Experts and Leading Authorities in their industry. She knows the importance of getting the right "visibility" to catapult your career from her past experience working in Corporate Finance. She teaches her clients how to strategically craft a game plan that gets them fast and customized results in their career trajectory. Nicole is part of the Esquire Coaching team.

Website: NicoleKLundy.com
Facebook: facebook.com/officialnkl
Twitter: @nicoleklundy

Chapter 3
The Purposeful Wardrobe:
Building Your Practice in Three Easy Pieces
by Nancy Barrood, Esq.

As a legal professional, you have already committed to living your life with purpose. Whether to help clients plan how their estates will be distributed after they pass, or helping to resolve marital issues, to negotiating intricate corporate deals, you have dedicated a significant portion of your life to reaching this point. You have dreamed of the day you would be licensed to fulfill your destiny, invested a significant amount of money, and countless hours of study to fulfilling your purpose. You have dreamed of your target client and worked to acquire the skills to earn their trust and confidence in you. Why not dress your body to reflect that?

First impressions matter. According to *Psychology Today*, you have three seconds to make a first impression. In three seconds, people have already formed an opinion about your competence to handle their particular legal issue.

You may be asking yourself, "Three seconds?" A lifetime of preparation only to be judged in three seconds? What could anyone possibly learn about me in three seconds?

Glad you asked.

There is only one possible character trait that anyone could learn about you in three seconds, and that is your personal appearance. In a word, style.

As a young, newly minted attorney, I appeared in court one day for oral argument on a motion of some importance to my client. It was particularly important for me, too, as it was one of my first. Full of the arrogance of recently acquired legal writing and research skills, I strode into the courtroom, with a barely used briefcase (read law school graduation gift), in hand. I was dressed, as you might imagine, in a combination of what I could afford, and the way I thought female attorneys dressed. My feet were aching in uncomfortable yet sturdy pumps, and my blue suit and plain white blouse were off the sale rack at the mall. I thought it fit well, but by the time I started oral argument, the back of the skirt had twisted to the front. Since this was my first time in this particular court house, I was disoriented, did not allow time to trek from the third floor of the parking deck down to the lobby of the courthouse, through security behind what seemed to be every litigant and their attorney in the district, back up to the third floor of the courthouse, and to the appropriate courtroom. Needless to say, by the time I arrived at my destination, I was nervous, disheveled and, yes, sweating.

As I made my way into the courtroom, there, almost angelic with the dusty sunlight filtering through the window of the courtroom, the crude shape of a halo shining off of his bald pate, stood my adversary. He was joking with the court clerk about the judge's golf game last weekend. My knees started to go weak and I felt a little nauseous. Before I half-blacked out, I noticed his French cuffs peeking oh so perfectly out of the cuff of his perfectly tailored navy gabardine suit, his shoes shone to perfection, a small pocket square folded artistically and perfectly in the breast pocket of his suit. Perfect.

The balance of the morning was a combination of the distant echo of the judge's voice in the distance, drowned out by the pounding of my head. Can you imagine that I was playing catch-up before oral argument started? That veteran attorney had mastered that all important first impression. And he used it to full advantage.

It was that day that I decided to make a study of my colleagues and how their physical appearance and personal style impacted their success. The guidelines I am about to share with you reflect a quarter century's experience observing my colleagues, fellow legal professionals, in all areas of practice, from matrimonial to bankruptcy, corporate attorneys to real estate professionals, as well as my own personal experience in litigation, mediation and contract negotiations. In observing my peers, the commonality among them is that their personal style always gave the first clue to their competence, manner and confidence in representing their clients. I am sharing my opinions, and invite you to use what is applicable to you and your practice.

Style Versus Fashion

Personal style is more than just clothing. It is not fashion. Think of fashion as trend, fad, and the stuff on the cover of Vogue. You will not, nor would you want to, see fashion walking down the street. Personal style, however, is in the magic of a handwritten thank you note in an electronic age; a firm and warm handshake; the subtlety of body language and eye contact, and yes, the flair of a scarf worn askew or the wraparound cuff links you found in a vintage store.

Of course, the grooming rituals we may have neglected in law school are now front and center. As an attorney, you are perceived as detail-oriented, given to precision in thinking and action. It stands to reason that your prospective client expects that detail to be reflected in your grooming. If your hair is sloppy or out of style or your fingernails are chipped, you are starting your relationship with your potential client at a disadvantage. Consider regular professional attention to your hair and fingernails as a necessary investment in your future.

Sales

Like it or not, as attorneys, we are all in sales. After all, what are sales? Convincing someone that his or her problem is going to be solved with our answer. Every moment of every day, we are sales people. From convincing a potential new client that we are the right firm to solve their problem, to advocating a position in court, to settling a case, to writing a brief, we are in sales. Our success depends on our ability to sell our position, and then to make sure our clients follow through and deliver on what we promised.

Recognizing and embracing that concept is the first step to using the techniques that sales people use to your best effect.

My favorite sales technique is a very popular one called 'mirroring'. You probably already do it and are not aware of it. Did you ever have someone come into your office for an initial consultation, and there is something unusual about the way they spoke? Did you find yourself subtly mimicking their tone or mannerisms? Most people do this instinctively. You may have also noticed that that person responded to you in a surprisingly positive way. That, in a nutshell, is mirroring, and it is a very effective tool when used in a conscious manner. People want to see something of themselves in those they trust to represent their interests.

Since your potential client will usually see you before they hear your voice, listen to your reasoning, or shake your hand, you have one chance to make that all-important first impression: your style. It is fairly easy to reflect a little of your desired clientele in your dress. That does not mean that you must lose your personality. If you are marketing yourself to a conservative client, such as an estate planning client, pull out that cameo from Great Aunt Ethel, and put it on a funky necklace, or find a vintage or consignment shop that will call you when they get a great pair of wraparound cufflinks. These were very popular in the 1950s, and are very elegant when worn with a wonderfully fitting French cuff shirt.

If you are representing corporate clientele, special attention to elegance must be paid. Corporate executives are used to paying for quality, and expect it to be reflected in the professionals around them. You must pay particular attention to detail and quality of fabric in your clothing.

In other words, know your target clientele and dress to show that you respect who they are and what they expect of you. A beautifully tailored suit in an elegant fabric is always a great choice, which leads me to your first "easy piece."

Easy Piece #1: The Perfect Suit

For men, the perfect suit is so easy, it is almost idiot-proof. I say 'almost' because there are some very easy pitfalls that many male shoppers fall into. Most men do not enjoy shopping for suits. I have met many men who send their wives or significant others to pick them out. It is a nasty chore that needs to get done. This is a mistake, as your wife cannot appear for fittings in your place or express your personality. So please, gentlemen, go in person. You might enjoy the attention. After the first time, your sales people will court you and the tailor will know you, and it will get that much easier to dress yourself appropriately.

Just because you get one free does not mean you want one free. There is a popular men's store which promises two free suits for every one you buy. What would your clients think of you if you offered them two free hours of your time for every one they paid for? As attorneys, we all seem to echo the mantra 'You get what you pay for'. I think it is safe to say that we have all given our share of free legal advice, whether to drive business by offering free initial consults, or because someone picked our brains at a cocktail party. How did that feel? Did that person appreciate the free advice you so generously offered or did they discount it as drivel since they were not paying you a fair rate for your knowledge and expertise?

Please remember that you are making an investment in a piece of clothing which will serve you twice per week for the next several years, if well cared for. Do not be shy about asking for help. First, choose a reputable retailer with a tailor on the premises. Successful men's wardrobes are accomplished professionals who make a nice living educating their clients on fit, fabric and color, because they then earn customer trust and loyalty, which translates into repeat business year after year. Let your sales person educate you, but if you seem to know more than they do about this topic, run, do not walk, out of the store.

For female attorneys, the pitfalls are more numerous. First, we have no uniform. Men walk into their favorite shop and buy their three essential suits twice per year, the tailor is ready to 'tweak' and off they go. That is why women fall into the first trap: What I like to call the 'men in skirts' trap. In our desire to have the perfect go-to, we apply the male rules to ourselves. What does that look like? Men in skirts. There is a reason, ladies, that we are the peacock of the species. We are not meant to wear the uniform. Have you ever noticed the ratio of women's clothing stores to men's in your local mall? Macy's devotes 75 percent of their store to women's clothing. They have a men's department.

If we are not men in skirts, what does our suit look like? During the 1970s and 1980s, when women were starting to crack the glass ceiling, the suit looked like a men's suit with a skirt attached. As female power in the workforce rose, we did not yet have the confidence to match, so we donned the 'big shoulder' look, apparently to beef up our appearance and make ourselves look more fierce, just as puffer fish do when threatened.

Women are now at a point where they do not need to 'puff themselves up' to look like more than we are. Women are finally realizing that they are already more without having to mimic men in their fashion. You are strong and confident, and you can show some personal style without sacrificing credibility. That does not, however, mean that you can raid our teenage daughter's closet and be taken seriously.

There is a fine line between dressing with style and being unprofessional. So, what does the perfect suit look like for the female legal professional? The answers are as numerous as there are women attorneys. There are, however, some general guidelines which will serve you well.

First, if you are the least bit unsure of whether a piece of clothing is appropriate, choose quality over a bargain every time. Shop at a store where you will receive personal attention, has choices that you like and can afford, and a sales clerk who will call you when your favorite pieces go on sale. Seek out the professional sales person who seems knowledgeable about their product and is willing to educate you on the best color and cut for your body type. Do not buy from the sales clerk who tells you how wonderful everything looks on you. I do not trust sales people who will not tell me, at least once during my fitting room experience, to "take that off."

Second, remember that a woman's suit does not have to be two matching pieces. A great woman's suit can be a tweed jacket with a solid wool trouser or skirt, a check skirt with a solid jacket, or even "soft suiting," which consists of a flowy sweater with a high quality gabardine trouser. These are pieces that you can mix and interchange in your wardrobe to make several different outfits.

Third, get a tailor. Clothing manufacturers do not know your particular body type, nor do they want to. All size eights do not have the same inseam. All size fourteens do not have the same arm length. To think that we are going to sail into our favorite store and fit perfectly into everything in our size is impractical. All well-dressed professionals need a tailor for a tweak now and again. Unfortunately, most women's clothing retailers do not have seamstresses or tailors on staff, but your local dry cleaner is a good place to start looking for a great tailor.

Finally, steal this tip from the boys: do not be afraid to repeat an outfit that works a couple of times during the week. A switch of scarf or blouse is all that is needed to make that investment suiting a workhorse.

Easy Piece #2: A Great Shoe Will Take You Places

Most male attorneys I have met over the years know the power of a good dress shoe, and are used to paying for this type of quality. You know that people look at your shoes first. But there are some of you who are not paying attention. Two or three pairs of dress shoes will serve you many years. Be certain that you own a pair of black and a pair of brown. If there is room in your budget, oxblood, a rich almost burgundy color, is a beautiful addition as it will mix well with everything in your closet. Gentlemen, the rule about your belt matching your shoes still applies, so be certain that you purchase a matching belt with your new shoes. And, above all, keep them polished. Nothing will deflate a client's confidence in you quicker than scuffed or worn looking shoes.

Recently, I presented at a meeting of very empowered, driven and accomplished female attorneys. The meeting itself was inspiring, full of the exchange of lofty ideas. At the end of the evening, after the audience had left, those women who had presented at the meeting were chatting. The topic of conversation? "Boy that was great, but I cannot wait to take off these heels." Ladies, imagine what you could accomplish if your feet didn't hurt. Why do you think the expression is "thinking on your feet", not "thinking on your high heels"? So frequently, we are driven by the lure of a bargain so that we can have several pairs of shoes instead of a couple of really high quality pairs that look professional without being dowdy. Please invest the time and a little extra money in finding the shoe that not only complements you but fits you so that you can invest that brain power in practicing law first, not worrying about your throbbing feet.

Easy Piece #3: Accessories Tell the Tale

We have talked about the concept of mirroring as a sales tool in building your practice. Your clients want to see a little bit of themselves in you.

But you want your clients to know a little bit about you, to feel that you have something in common, and one of the most intimate ways to reveal something about yourself is through your accessories.

Do not underestimate the power of subtlety. A little goes a long way. If you are passionate about horses, for example, by all means wear the silk scarf with the equestrian motif or the tie pin in the shape of a horseshoe. Do not cover yourself in horse paraphernalia, however, or you will look clownish.

In my office on any given day, you are likely to see me wearing pearls in some form or other. Because of my love of the ocean and disdain for blind conformity, I am always on the lookout for accessories that use pearls in unusual and interesting ways. This is a great conversation starter with new clients, and returning clients are always interested in my latest find.

A Word About Color

Throughout history, color has been very powerfully tied to results. A working knowledge of color and its effect on your clients and adversaries is critical to your choice of wardrobe for your day.

When you are choosing your clothing for the day, think about your schedule. What do you want to accomplish and who are you meeting? The colors you choose to wear that day will depend on your purpose.

Why is our society so strongly tied to white as the standard color for wedding dresses? We associate white with purity and innocence, for new beginnings. Our doctors wear white coats to instill in their patients a sense of cleanliness and good health. White dress shirts are always a good way to start any outfit, for men and women. White is the "tabula rasa," or clean slate which starts us off on our day. You probably do not want to wear white, or any one color, from head to toe.

Red has long been associated with power. Red is intimidating, and can be associated with danger. Think of a stop sign or a barber's pole. This is a great color to wear in the courtroom to gain advantage over an adversary, but not to settle a case. If you enjoy wearing red often, consider tempering it with black.

If you are involved in a mediation or settlement negotiations, you may want to choose a pastel tie or blouse. There is a reason we have colors with names like 'baby blue' and 'powder puff pink'. These are colors associated with innocence, purity and reason. You will be perceived as the voice of reason in the room.

Purple is interesting as it is perceived as a sign of wealth and royalty. If this is the perception you are after for the day, do not hesitate to wear purple. But use purple sparingly, as this color is also associated with great sadness.

Black, of course, is the great neutral that can be read in a variety of ways. Wearing black head to toe can be perceived as evil. Unless that is your goal, be certain to temper black with less threatening colors. If you are trying to drive home a point which has no middle ground, black and white is your combination, hence the term.

Do not feel that you must be ruled by color. This is simply a guide to make you aware of the subtle effects certain colors have on those around you. Please do wear and enjoy the colors which complement you and in which you feel most comfortable. When in doubt, close your eyes. How does the color you are wearing make you feel? Are you feeling peaceful or agitated? Empowered or distressed? Be guided by your own impressions and trust your instincts. If your outfit makes you feel happy, you will project that and those around you will feel that happiness.

Finally, be confident. Once you have invested in your key, well-fitting and high quality pieces, take a good long look in the mirror at the accomplished, amazing professional that you are. You worked long and hard to arrive at this place. You know you have the skills to serve the clients you desire, and you look the part. Smile, knowing that you now have all the tools necessary to make a great first impression, and that will allow your clients to see the brilliance within.

About Nancy Barrood, Esq.

Nancy Barrood, Esq., is a personal stylist for attorneys and is part of the Esquire Coaching team. During her 20-year tenure practicing law, Nancy documented how wardrobe choices affected her colleagues. She believes that advocacy begins with first impressions, and she has been helping her colleagues achieve more effective outcomes by first building their own confidence, coaching attorneys to dress to persuade, be conciliatory, command the room, or attract new clients. Nancy also owns Buttons and BowTies.

Website: etcetera.com
Website: jhilburn.com
Facebook: facebook.com/nancy.barrood;
Facebook: facebook.com/ButtonsBowsByNancyBarrood
LinkedIn: linkedin.com/pub/nancy-barrood/7/b48/990

Chapter 4
Content Leadership:
A Powerful Marketing Position
by Margo DeGange, M.Ed.

Not long ago, marketing your law practice was in a way, all about you. It meant advertising and promoting your services and products so you could gain a client. Once you did, the relationship began.

Today, the relationship begins well before anyone ever becomes a client, and marketing is now mostly all about them.

Nowadays, they have more control, and they want more than just products and services. They want people they can trust.

The way you will gain a client today is to stand for something he or she resonates with and believes in—to have a business purpose so meaningful that it penetrates the hearts and minds of your prospects and permeates their lives.

No more is your brand simply a logo and a color. It is now a way of thinking about, relating to, and interacting with your world. Your brand is your business world-view and philosophy (and it better be good!). (See Chapter 2 for more on branding.)

So, instead of creating clients, today you create subscribers—people who you sincerely want to help. They subscribe to your business philosophy (your brand), because they know that. Although you are a lawyer, your real job is to be a marketer. As a modern–day marketer who happens to be a lawyer, you do this through communication.

Today's savvy marketer is not selling, manipulating, or pushing, but communicating valuable content that subscribers want, need, look for, and enjoy. That's good, because most people don't readily trust content that comes from brands, as they assume they are being "sold to," and most of the time, they are right.

This means, you have an enormous opportunity here to flourish and thrive, and to become an influential thought leader instead of a product pusher. Your tribe of subscribers should look to you as an expert and important resource for the information they see as relevant, making you an important part of their lives.

Showing Up as a Leader

You don't come to the scene as a know-it-all, self promoter, or diva with something for the masses. You also don't come with a slew of biased content on the back end of a barrage of links. Showing up as a leader means you know precisely who you are leading. You know them well, and you fully understand and care about their concerns. You know them so well that you know how to help them get where they need to be. This is the only way they will trust you.

A leader is propelled by a purpose, a mission, a "story" that others are inspired by (your brand). You lead by creating and distributing relevant, high quality content that stems from your story (brand), and that's designed specifically to help a clearly defined target audience.

Through meaningful content, you become someone people want to listen to and follow because you're a trusted specialist with advice and information they seek. They recognize your expertise, and sense that you have their best interests at heart.

If you want to market effectively and profitably, become a relationship builder and a leader, with a content-driven marketing approach, and a plan that's easy to manage. Present your audience with consistent, compelling content they associate with your brand. Entertain them with your stories, engage them with your ideas, and educate them with your insights. Inspire them and move them to action. A sales-pitch just won't do that!

Attracting Your Community

A legal practice must have clients. Clients are attracted to certain businesses, but not others, and although you may not share all of the personal details of your passion and purpose with your tribe, the essence of it should be communicated throughout your brand. This intentional messaging is what attracts the right clients to you and helps you build a thriving, robust community. If your purpose rings true to others, they are likely to become your clients.

Your Personal Commitment and Connection to Your Work

Content marketing actually begins with you. Before knowing why you are practicing law, know who you are, and how the work you do adds richness—not just money—to your personal life. From there you discover what your bigger purpose is within and through your work. Who do you influence or impact? How, and why? What is the significance of your work to the bigger picture of life in general? This is the underlying motivation of your brand that stems from you. Intimately know and embrace this motivation. Then, make a commitment to always serve yourself and others from this vantage point. Be committed to your purpose!

In other words, know why you chose your practice group or business, and let this be the cause others rally around (the story). From there, you simply communicate, demonstrate, substantiate, reiterate, and authenticate this cause in every aspect of your content marketing.

The Long Haul: Content Marketing—A Business Lifestyle

Before you even think about going anywhere on the content marketing train, know that you are the conductor, not the passenger. That means you don't get off at any of the stops. You keep on riding the train—indefinitely! Content marketing is actually a mindset more than it is a marketing strategy. Plan to make it a business way of life.

Content Marketing Tactics: How You Interact and Share

Becoming a leader and an informative resource in your niche takes planning. You need a content marketing strategy, with specific tactics along with a schedule that works for both you and your audience. With that stated, you should also know that in the midst of your plan, a certain amount of randomness and spontaneity will be a part of the mix.

Now let's get to the meat and potatoes of the tactics involved in a content marketing strategy. There are a number of vehicles you can use to get the stories and information in front of your community. The ones you choose will depend on your goals and your available resources such as time, staff, and dollars. There isn't a template for all business owners. This is a custom job! Find what works best for you, and build and tweak as you go. As an important reminder, be sure to adhere to all attorney advertising rules when engaging in any marketing activities.

Be committed to a business lifestyle that embraces content marketing as a long-term endeavor. It's not the kind of thing you start and stop. Writing a blog post here and there, publishing an article without a plan, and randomly posting on social networks is quite possibly a total waste of time, and it definitely is not content marketing.

Your Business Card

I start the list with the simple business card because it can actually become a content piece for prospects. You probably give cards out regularly, so why not set the tone of your content-leadership brand by placing a quick tip or meaningful quote on your card? This hints to others that you just might be an informative resource, rather than a hungry salesperson! Be sure your card displays your fabulous, purpose-driven logo that actually tells a story. You may have opportunity to expound on that story at some future point.

Your E-Mail Signature

When you send or reply to an e-mail, you have prime real estate to communicate a purpose-driven message that prospects can relate to. Instead of using this space to brag about your credentials, communicate the essence of your brand with a few words or key statements about how you help change lives for the better. Keep it short and attractive. Offer a piece of highly useful content—through a link in the signature—that will appeal to your target client. Get them to take an action that builds trust. Never yuck up your signature with too many links or accolades of how great you are. Instead, make it clear you are showing up right there with a way to help them! Be clear about the beneficial action you want them to take as well. Include your full name and basic contact information.

Your Free Gift on a Website or Landing Page

This tactic ties in perfectly with your e-mail signature, because the link I recommend you put in your signature will lead them to a landing page where they do just one thing: fill out a form for that *Valuable Free Gift*.

Again, this gift will be some type of highly useful content that is relevant to your ideal clients. It can be a report, a checklist, a *Top Ten List*, a *Mistakes to Avoid* article, an audio, or anything that helps them solve an issue, reduce discomfort, or increase happiness in some way (and the name of the free gift should clearly represent that).

Your *Valuable Free Gift* is your first significant opportunity to begin a relationship with your prospect and communicate a clear message and a meaningful purpose tied to your story and brand. Show up here as a leader and knowledgeable expert. They will really appreciate your generosity.

Keep this landing page clean and clear of clutter. Display only your photo, your logo, the name of the report, and the signup form. There should not be tabs, articles, or any other offers on this page. This is not your website. This page has one purpose and function—to get them signed up for your gift. In the e-mail confirmation and the gift they receive, you will tell them about your website where they can learn more about you, your brand, your overriding purpose, and your mission to help them.

Here's a big tip: since the prospect doesn't likely know you when they arrive at your page for the gift, only ask for their first name and e-mail address or you risk scaring them away. Also make it clear they are signing up for your e-mail list. Now you have their blessing to communicate with them going forward.

Your SEO

Search Engine Optimization (SEO) is the foundation of your content strategy, because it helps your content reach more people and helps prospects to find you.

Let's keep this simple: create a list of 15-25 key words and key phrases your target client would likely use online to search for the solutions they need. Think from their point of view, not yours. Include in your list the geographic regions you service and the type of law you practice. Update this list periodically. Use Google Tools to do a key word search of words your target clients use in searches.

Then, create content that is useful, rich, and informative, and not filled with URLs and self promotion. Write so that your key words and phrases show up throughout each piece. Here's the key though: don't stuff your content with key words for the sake of key words, as this can hurt your online rankings. Write naturally. If some of your key words fit the content, great. Once you complete your writing, go back and see where you can include additional key words in a way that flows well.

Titles are fabulous places for key phrases. The titles of your blog posts, articles, videos, webpages, and other content should always include important key words.

See that each page of your website has good title tags and descriptions (which will be indexed in search engines).

If you want to come up in local searches, take a few minutes to add your business to Google+ Local. There's no charge, and the benefits are many.

Visit relevant blogs and news sights related to your niche area, and comment on posts where your insight would be beneficial. Include a link back to your website. Google Alerts is a wonderful tool to flag specific topics about which you want to be notified. If a relevant post shows up online containing your Google Alert word or phrase, Google will notify you by e-mail. Then you can go to that site and post a comment that includes your website link.

Your Newsletter or Ezine

Regular communication that your tribe can count on is golden. Send a weekly or monthly e-mail newsletter to your list. (This list includes those who signed up for your *Valuable Free Gift*, and your current and past clients.)

You can be the cool lawyer, the interesting lawyer, or the funny lawyer, but whatever you do, don't be the boring lawyer. Keep your newsletters short and sweet, with punchy subject lines that get your readers excited and ready to see what great things you have to say "this time." Include a concise but enticing article and a tip, plus your photo with a short bio. You can also keep subscribers up to date on events of interest.

Your newsletter is a great tool for referral marketing, especially if your content is solid. Make it easy for Joe or Kim to forward your newsletter to a friend. Include social media and "forward to a friend" links.

Your Blog

Your blog can be a fabulous resource for prospects. Wordpress is an SEO-friendly platform that allows you to have a blog right on your website, with custom categories you create, that help visitors search your site.

Set up five to eight strategic topic categories in advance. Every time you create a blog post, choose just one category to link it to. This helps you focus on the topic so you give solid information every time you write. The categories then become powerful search tools.

Aim for a blog post of about 250-300 words. Ditch the "fluff" so each post is brimming with richness.

Blog once a week—consistently (or more often if you have the time or the staff). Pull excerpts from your articles or books, or expand on a social media post you've written, reworking it so it's somewhat different from content you've posted elsewhere.

Your blog is where you can shine as a leader. Be interesting, informative, fun, and educational. Posts can include your thoughts on relevant news stories and legal issues, tips your readers will enjoy, what's happening in your community, upcoming events you're hosting, pertinent lifestyle information, and testimonials on occasion. (See Chapter 6 for more blogging strategies.)

Every blog post should have social media buttons for easy sharing.

Your Guest Blog Appearances

Guest blogging is when you write a post for a blog other than your own. This has lots of SEO love since your post will link back to your website (called a backlink). As you make connections in online and offline communities, see where you can offer to guest blog. Aim for the most desirable blogs to get the best bling for your time-investment buck. Ask colleagues if you can share a post on their blog.

Your article or post does not have to be lengthy or full of legal jargon. It just needs to be helpful, entertaining, inspiring, or educational. A solid (key word rich) paragraph or two will do the trick!

Have you ever commented to an online post only to be represented by an impersonal, grey Avatar? The solution is to visit the free site, Gravatar.com, where you can upload your photo or logo. Then whenever you post on blogs, your photo and backlink automatically show up.

Your Digital Magazine

Basically, a digital magazine is a glorified PDF with text and images. People are drawn to them since they are often attractive and bold.

You can publish a simple digital magazine of your own that totally appeals to your desired prospect and send it out quarterly or even twice a year. It doesn't have to be a big deal. Send it to everyone on your list, and have a way for people to sign up for it for free on your website! This has tremendous value, and I'll bet hardly any lawyer is doing this. You can hire a graphic designer, or create your magazine in a program as basic as Word.

Here's a simple plan: for each issue, write the main article. Select a few "featured writers" to contribute articles your list would be interested in reading, such as time management, office organization, or creating strong family relationships. Eight to twelve articles per issue is plenty.

Keep your magazine clean and unfussy, with an image and a title for the cover, along with some highlights of what's inside. Pick one attractive graphic per article. Use your own photos or purchase royalty-free images for a very low price. There's no need to get extravagant. Your magazine can even be less than 30 pages!

There are free services out there that will turn your Word document into a PDF, and host your magazine, so all you have to do is share the link with your readers. You just upload your doc and share. Check out issuu.com to see some examples.

Your Articles

You can and should write articles pertaining to your area of the law. Article marketing can be a tremendous lead source.

Write both locally and nationally. Homeowners associations and clubs often look for experts to write in their newsletters. Local newspapers are also a source. Lawyers can offer tips on creating a will, starting a business, or navigating changing family dynamics. Many topics of interest to the community overlap into your area of specialty.

Article directory sites such as EzineArticles.com make it easy for you to become an expert online. Droves of people read these articles, and share them on their blogs, citing the author's information. Every Ezine Article features a resource box where you can place a link, and every EzineArticles.com author has their bio and photo featured on the Ezine Articles website. Everything you write for them links to this bio, and also links back to your site.

Your Articles don't have to be long. You can create content that is clean and simple. The important thing is to make each article useful and beneficial so the reader wants to reach out to you for more great content. Have a main goal for each article: where will you send the reader after they read your content (perhaps to a landing page for report related to the article)? Focus the writing of each article on one major topic, with three sub points to support it, and a clear call to action.

The same SEO and key word rules apply here as were mentioned above.

Your Speaking

Speaking engagements are a fabulous way to add value to the community and inadvertently market your services. Many local, regional, and even national clubs and organizations seek knowledgeable expert speakers. You can secure speaking engagements—particularly local gigs—to create awareness of your services in your community.

Match your audience to your topic, and you could win big. For instance, if you do wills and estate planning, you could speak at assisted living centers and hospital senior clubs.

Host regularly scheduled events such as a Lunch and Learn for prospects and for your past and current clients. This keeps you fresh on their minds. These seminars should be fun, highly interesting, and useful. List the upcoming topics on your website under "events." Invite attendees through your newsletter, and encourage them to bring a friend.

At the end of every speech, offer the audience a low risk way to connect further with you (or work with you). Have a way for them to sign up for your *Valuable Free Gift* (e-mail list), too.

Your Social Media

Invest a few minutes daily on social media sites like Facebook, Twitter, and LinkedIn, but have a clear strategy when you do. Social media can be a time waster if you have no plan.

Share inspirational messages and images that encourage and support others. Work to build a community of individuals who see you as a thought leader and expert in your field who is helpful, personable, caring, and accessible. Allow plenty of time to build relationships.

Provide value. Don't dump business links or promote your business outside of a clear context. Be a positive and friendly resource, and stay clear of debates and negative interaction.

Search social media sites for local people you would like to know, and connect with them online. Take the relationship further by meeting for coffee. Use social media as a relationship-building tool. It's so powerful to go to a local event, and have a "stranger" approach you and say they "know" you from Facebook. It's a great way to form solid bonds.

Your Videos

Don't shy away from video. It's the best way—in terms of content—for your audience to experience your personality fully.

Video marketing is easy if you implement a schedule. Create a video each month—That's 12 per year—which is way better than none! Dress your best, smile, make it about them, and give great information.

Select one topic for each video, and stick with it all the way through. Begin with a quick but warm welcome, add an informative middle, and conclude with a call to action. Do all this in one to four minutes.

Post your videos to YouTube and Vimeo, and then you can blog about them, embedding the link in your blog or website. Tweet and post the video or blog link, adding a sentence or two of how it will help your subscribers.

Video will do great things for your SEO, since Google adores this kind of content. It will help you reach the first page on Google searches. That's a wrap!

Your Book

Write a book! As a content marketer and author, I write books. As a book publisher and content marketing coach, I publish books for professionals and business owners, and this I know: probably the single most significant thing you can do to appear as a notable expert is to author a book.

Authors get invited to important events and get speaking engagements easier and more frequently than non-authors. By writing a book you gain instant respect, and a clear, competitive advantage.

Start writing your book. This can be one you co-author with one or a few others or a book you author alone. You probably have content that can become a book, such as audios that can be transcribed, or speech notes that can be expanded. If you're starting from scratch, write about top concerns your target client might have on a certain subject. You can be the expert and leader who address those concerns with wisdom and authority.

Don't put off this important content marketing step. I love helping my clients create their books, because I see what a huge confidence booster it is for them, and how quickly it takes them to the next level. If you need help with the book writing and publishing process, I am here to help. The point is . . . just write your book!

Same Outfit, New Accessories

Content marketing requires you to offer a constant flow of content to your community, including information on current news and trends, interesting stories, inspirational pieces, and everyday useful tips and advice. Some of these can be created by repurposing what you already have.

If you've written an article, break it down into 100 tweets, or 12 Facebook posts. Your seminar handouts can become a checklist. With a few more sentences, a Facebook response could be your next blog post.

Get as many uses out of each piece of content as possible, planning some of this repurposing in advance.

My biggest tip here: don't duplicate information over different channels, particularly online. Google frowns on that, and it could hurt your search rankings. If you post an article in one place, change it up slightly when you post it somewhere else. If you use an excerpt from your book on your blog, for example, add a few new words and a different heading.

Think of the content you have as the classic little black dress: a few new accessories, and no one knows you've already worn it.

Time for Action: A Simple Schedule to Make it All Work

Do you need a simplified content marketing plan? Here's one for you: pick the activities from the list below that you want to implement, and schedule them on your calendar well in advance, using the frequency suggestions I recommend (below). Pre-write some of the content once you know your publishing dates (you can increase the frequency or the number of outlets, but if you do, make sure you can be consistent). Then get going, even if you have to start small and slow, because a simple plan beats no plan at all.

Finally, don't hesitate to let me know how you are coming along as the new content leader in your professional niche.

Your Simple Content Marketing Schedule

Newsletter—Publish it monthly or weekly. (Plan the year's topics and images in advance.)

Blog Posts—Publish one post weekly with an image. (Plan the year's topics in advance.)

Guest Blog—Do one per month. (Secure guest posts in advance and then plan the topics.)

Digital Magazine—Publish it two to four times annually. (Plan the year in advance. Predetermine themes, topics, titles, images, and guest writers.) Here's a great tip: use your digital magazine as your Valuable Free Gift.

Articles—Publish monthly. (Plan the year's topics in advance.)

Speaking Engagements—Secure two per month. (Create your signature speech and one additional speech related to your practice area and filled with benefits for the audience.)

Free Seminars—Host one weekly. This can be a Lunch and Learn. (Plan the year's topics and handouts in advance.)

Social Media—Post on two to three major sites daily. (Use a combination of repurposed content, excerpts that you reword, fresh content, and real-time interactivity. Create some of the posts in advance. Use scheduling software like HootSuite to automate and manage social media.)

About Margo DeGange

"Biz-ibility" Expert and International Best-Selling Author & Speaker Margo DeGange, M.Ed. is a Business & Lifestyle Designer, and founder of Women of Splendor, the exciting mentoring organization where spiritually-minded women collaborate to become wildly successful. Quarterly, Margo hosts the celebrated and life-transforming Women of Splendor 4-Seasons of Success conferences. Margo is founder of Splendor Publishing, helping entrepreneurs get published and bring their life-changing messages to others. She'll help you discover your "Gift of Brilliance" and communicate it so you "Shine Full Throttle!"

Website: MargoDegange.com
Website: SplendorPublishing.com
Website: WomenOfSplendor.com
Facebook: facebook.com/margo.degange
LinkedIn: linkedin.com/in/margodegange
Twitter: @margodegange
Twitter: @splendorpublish
Twitter: @womenofsplendor

Chapter 5
Don't Sell Yourself. Be Yourself: Strategies for Authentic Networking
by Jennifer Robinson, Esq.

I used to be a litigator for large insurance companies. I did not have to generate my own client base; my clients were policyholders. I did see how difficult it was for friends and colleagues to generate their own clients and leads. Time is at a premium. More importantly, we were not taught how to build relationships or makes sales in law school. Even if you do not have to generate your own book of business or you stop practicing law altogether, you need to be able to build, maintain and sustain a network. It should be mandatory coursework. I left practicing law after 12 years in litigation and have had to teach myself how to network as an entrepreneur. I would not say I was a typical "stay in my lane" type of lawyer, which has probably served me well as an entrepreneur. For all of you still in the profession, I'd like to provide some tips to make your professional and personal life easier and happier by connecting, giving and being your authentic self.

Put Yourself Out There

I cannot stress the importance of this enough when you are trying to build a business. People have to know who you are and what you do in order to do business with you and recommend you to others. This is not something that occurs simply by having a strong social media presence or putting an ad in a newspaper. In fact, I generally do not subscribe to paying for marketing. There are too many lawyers out there and you need to find a way to distinguish yourself. Of course you should join both your local and national bar organizations, but those are groups for lawyers and it is not enough. Try to join more diverse networking groups and associations where there are people from all professions and walks of life, especially where your ideal client may be. If you can find some with exclusivity by industry, this is even better. For example, BNI (Business Network International) only accepts one person per industry. So if you are a family lawyer for example and join a BNI chapter, no other family lawyer can join that chapter and people in your chapter have agreed to refer to members of that chapter. In this manner, you can't help but get business. But also look at joining your local rotary or chamber of commerce and attending events regularly (or even hosting one at your office) to get to know those people in your local community that will be able to refer you to others. Finally, think about teaching or speaking locally, even if it is unpaid. Think of it as a marketing budget and a way to gain a "warm intro" into a new group of people you can get to know and in turn, they can get to know you and your business.

Be a Listener and Be a Giver

When you go out to events, do not simply hand out cards. In fact, I rarely hand out my cards unless someone asks for it or there is a specific reason to follow up. Going to an event with a goal of giving out 25 cards is not a good use of the time you set aside for networking. Instead, go with the goal of meeting three to five people and having meaningful conversations. These conversations are not an opportunity to sell yourself and your services. They are an opportunity for you to get to know as much as you can about your new acquaintance and also an opportunity to be memorable. Sure, you should be ready to discuss what you do briefly and to hear what they do, but it is more important to listen to who they are and what they need. Try to find affinity or common ground with someone-maybe you both have young children, both play tennis, both just got engaged, both love dogs. Finding common ground makes it easier to open up and makes it easier to follow up with that person. Be listening for ways you can help the person you are speaking to with an intro to a potential partner or client. Even if you are a personal injury lawyer talking to another personal injury lawyer, you should not look at them as your competition, but instead look for ways you can collaborate with each other and partner. Maybe you could teach a seminar together. Maybe that attorney is someone who you could refer cases to that are conflicts for you or you cannot handle for other reasons. It is very useful and important to friend your competition and those in your industry as well as those outside your industry.

Be a Connector and Follow Up

When you come home from a networking event, make notes about the people you met or put their cards in a separate envelope and date it so you won't forget where you met them. Try to follow up with them in 24-48 hours if possible so the memory of who you are is fresh in their minds. This follow up could be a call, an e-mail or a personal note. These days, people receive so many e-mails in a day it helps you stand out to go a different route. When you reach out to them, remind them where you met and maybe what you discussed. For example, "It was great to meet you yesterday at the chamber event and talk to you about our love of traveling and your upcoming trip to China. I would love to meet for coffee when you return and hear about your trip and learn more about your business."

It is a good practice to make one-on-one meetings or phone calls with new people you meet to learn about how you can help each other. But this is not a scorecard; it is hopefully going to be a long-term and genuine relationship. Therefore, just because you do someone a favor or connect them with someone, do not assume "they owe you." Of course, all of us are in business to make money, but if you give with the expectation of getting something in return, this is not really giving – it is *expecting*. Know in your mind that you are banking your networking karma and that ultimately good things will come back to you. It may sound cliché, but I have found it to be very true. Certainly the converse is true—if you become known as someone who asks for favors and never helps anyone else out, over time no one will help you.

Finally, think about other things you can do to help someone you have met. Maybe an invite comes across your desk to an industry event you think they might enjoy. Invite them to go with you or even just forward the invitation to them. Perhaps you see an article about something you know they would be interested in. Forward it to them. These are things that take very little time, but are very much appreciated by others. It shows you were thinking about them and it also helps keep you in the forefront of their minds. Sending cards is also a great way to stay in touch. Instead of sending holiday cards that get lost in the shuffle of 50 other holiday cards, send out a card at a less trafficked time of year. For example, send a "Happy Spring" card or a birthday card.

Do Your Homework Before and After an Event or Conference: Be Strategic!

It is never a bad thing to simply talk to people at an event you naturally gravitate towards based on their energy and your instincts. However, if you are attending an important event or conference with a lot of prospects, you should have a plan. This plan starts before you arrive. Often times there are attendee lists that are accessible once you buy a ticket or RSVP. Look them over and see if there are a few people that you really would like to meet.

If this list is not available, call the event or conference planners and ask if there is such a list they could e-mail you.

Do your research. Look up your target attendees' LinkedIn profiles and websites. Research the latest things going on with their companies. Read their blog or newsletter if they have them. Be prepared! Additionally, while you never want to "pitch" someone you meet for the first time, be ready with a 30-second pitch to advise what you do in a succinct manner. Think about conversation starters based on your research. Maybe the two of you both run marathons. Look for entry points that conversation will flow from naturally because the topic is one that you are both already interested and vested in. If you cannot find your target people at the event, ask the people at registration if they have checked in and if they can point them out or even introduce you. Or simply ask a few guests, "Do you know Jim Smith? I saw he was attending and would love to meet him. Can you point him out?"

Finally, be ready to answer what someone can do for you. This may not happen during a first conversation, but people cannot help you meet the right folks unless you tell them what you need. Be prepared with this response. For example, "I am looking to speak to some local community groups about the importance of having an estate plan." This will help them think about who in their own network might be a good connection for you to help make that happen.

Respect Referrals

If you are given an introduction or a referral, make sure you follow up in a timely manner. If someone in your network has done this for you, be respectful. Odds are they have told the person you will be contacting them and the more time that goes by, the worse you look. It is disrespectful. Even if it is a particularly busy week for you, a simple e-mail that says, "Thank you for connecting us. I have a big project due this week and am swamped, but I would love to set up a time next week to talk."

Be Consistent

I can't tell you how often I hear things like, "I went to an event of X organization, but didn't make any good connections, so I'm not going back" or "I've been going to those meetings for six months and nothing has come of it. I'm not going to go anymore." Business does not happen right away. It takes time for people to get to know you. It is also sometimes about being in the right place at the right time. You might go to ten monthly lunches and at the eleventh lunch the same person you've seen every month just lost a parent and needs an estate attorney. Sometimes it is about timing.

It is not enough to simply join an organization. I am active with my local chamber and sometimes I talk to people who tell me they are chamber members because they feel they should be, but have never attended an event. Or they attend one to two events a year. This is not the way to form relationships, particularly if you are in fields where there are a lot of people who do what you do. People will come to you because they have gotten to know you over time.

Self-Promotion is Not the Enemy

It is important to spread the word about what you are doing. Maybe you just went out on your own and opened your own practice. Maybe you are running a great promotion. Maybe you are going to be the keynote speaker at an important industry event. Share those things with your network and make sure you promote them through social media. If you develop strong relationships with people, they will want to see you succeed, and they will promote your news and happenings without you even asking them to do so. They will do this because they care about you.

Get Involved!

If you have your own practice or need to generate your own book of business, get involved! Volunteer for an organization that means something to you. Serve as a sponsor for a local charity run. Sit on a board. Join a book club. Join a committee at your church or other religious institution. These are all ways of networking as well. You will be working with people you already have things in common with. For example, if eradicating cancer is important to you and you volunteer with a cancer-related non-profit, other volunteers will sign up because this is also a priority for them. Getting involved in these types of activities also opens you up to people outside of your regular network and helps you meet new people. It is not enough to have a word-of-mouth business. You should always be looking to meet new people and expand your network.

Conclusion

I hope these tips will help you to build your professional and personal networks. In three years there has only been one event where I felt like I truly wasted my time attending (and I attend networking events or one-on-one meetings almost every day!). Most of the time, I meet wonderful and interesting people who I am happy to get to know and recommend. Social media and technology is great and definitely useful for maintaining contact with people over time, but never underestimate the power of in-person conversations. Happy Connecting!

About Jennifer Robinson, Esq.

Jennifer Lynn Robinson is CEO and Founder of Purposeful Networking. She consults with individuals to target their ideal clients through improved relationship building. She conducts workshops and speaking engagements for workplaces, business associations and other groups. Jennifer holds certifications in Event Planning, Non-Profit Management and Conflict Resolution. She received her B.A. from Haverford College and J.D. from Villanova. Jennifer lives with her husband and their three rescue dogs in suburban Philadelphia. She's also on the Esquire Coaching Team.

Website: PurposefulNetworking.com
Facebook: facebook.com/EventsWithAPurpose
Twitter: @AreYouNetworked

Chapter 6
Word-of-*Mouse* Referrals from Blogging
by Vikram Rajan

What is "word-of-*mouse*" marketing?

Have you ever been recommended to a new client or potential opportunity by e-mail? Perhaps a colleague has introduced you to someone by cc'ing you in an e-mail. Do you consider this a word-of-mouth referral or an Internet lead? Most likely, you'd call it word-of-mouth. But e-mail is an aspect of the Internet, no?

And so, the play on words: word-of-mouse marketing is word-of-mouth, enabled by the Internet. It's clearly different from what we typically regard as Internet marketing:

• Search Engine Optimization (SEO), or getting to the top of Google, etc.

• Or, Pay-Per-Click (PPC), like Google Adwords or even Facebook Ads.

• And of course e-mail introductions are quite different from website banner advertising, annoying popups, and pre-rolls (the ads that run right before you watch a video, on YouTube, Hulu, etc.) is alive inside me as I answer these questions?

Word-of-mouse marketing also happens through LinkedIn, its Groups, and other social media. After all, what's the big difference between being cc'd on an e-mail, and being introduced to someone via LinkedIn? What if someone learns about you through a LinkedIn profile, or sees a comment or post you make in a

LinkedIn Group? Sure, this sounds more and more like Internet marketing. But ultimately, these new contacts are trusting in you based on real-life (often mutual) relationships. This is what puts the *social* in social media.

Most law firms grow through what I call "passive" word-of-mouth. Referrals are the result of the goodwill generated by doing a good job for good people. It's natural and traditional. But what about all those relationships and people who forget about you?

Can you honestly remember every one of your potential clients, past clients and colleagues that you've e-mailed in the past two years? Well, if you can't remember them—and they were potential new business for you—how can we expect for them to remember you? And if they can't remember you, how can they recommend you or contact you when the time's right?

Thus, nowadays, word-of-mouth marketing ought to be more pro-active (rather than passive). This is why law firms send out newsletters, are promoting articles through LinkedIn Groups, Google+, Facebook and Twitter. This is why so many law firms are blogging. This is why the American Bar Association has been rating the Top 100 Lawyer Blogs (aka, the bLAWg 100) since 2007, dedicating its December cover of the ABA Journal ever since.

Lucrative referrals can be the result of strategic, pro-active initiatives. It begins greatly with your own blog. This fuels and aggregates what you do on LinkedIn, Avvo, JD Supra and related social media. Likewise, your blogging and social media are the content for your e-mail newsletter—the most common denominator of Internet marketing.

The hundreds, if not thousands, of relationships you've made are represented by the e-mail addresses in your Outlook, Gmail, Apple Mail, etc. As you remind them of your existence, expertise and excellence, they will come out of the woodwork with questions, seeking your help. It may be for them, for their loved ones, or for organizations to which they belong (their companies, professional associations, charities, etc.). They will likewise forward or share your blog articles and social media posts to colleagues, friends and even acquaintances. All of these are the Internet-based equivalent of referrals. These referrals are the result of your word-of-mouse marketing.

In my first book, 365 Marketing Thumb-rules: Daily Reminders for Rainmakers (available at marketingthumbrules.com), I highlight many do's and don'ts. For example, marketing follows nearly all the axioms of physical fitness: start small, consult professionals and always be consistent!

The following are short articles—edited from my own blog—to help you start and/or improve your own pro-active word-of-mouse marketing. I look forward to your questions, and your results.

E-mail me at vik@phoneBlogger.net.

26 Blog Article Ideas: the Brainstormer

One of the most frustrating aspects of blogging is thinking of new ideas. To help our clients, I used to use a column I wrote for the AICPA, CPA Insider newsletter; it had 20 ideas. In the years since, I have more blog post ideas; and more ways to come up with more article ideas.

So I'd like to present to you *26 Blog Article Ideas*, aka, our "Blog Brainstormer," available publicly at BrandedExpert.com. Feel free to share in its entirety. You'll see that this litany of ideas is broken down into four sections.

The best blog articles are written as though you're speaking with a potential client, or possibly a referral source. Naturally, your style would be conversational yet professional. Truly, your blog articles will mirror the *Frequently Asked Questions* (FAQ) you answer every day.

You may want to think about the questions and topics you've now become "bored" to answer or talk about: elementary subjects to you are often most relevant to your clients and referral sources. Remember, these 26 ideas can prompt multiple blog articles each.

Blog Article Idea Section 1: Branded Expert Articles Help Position You as a Thought Leader

1. Tell us about your latest or upcoming speaking engagement (or media reference).

2. What are two or three misconceptions about your field or practice?

3. Can you explain a popular acronym, jargon, or credential or visual diagram in your field?

4. Any new regulation, ruling, legislation or obligation affecting your field or clientele?

5. Any (recurring or upcoming) deadline, due date, or date-driven obligation?

6. Can you comment on an article or book [link] that's relevant to your expertise, profession, or clientele?

7. Have you learned anything new at a conference?

8. Tell us about a recent report or survey [link].

9. Any important dates or new trends to address? How does it affect your clientele?

10. Clients' other concerns (not directly addressed by your practice), but affects your advice, planning, etc.?

Blog Article Idea Section 2: Client FAQ Ideas Prompt Articles, with Questions You May Hear Asked by Clients, Potential Clients, and Referral Sources

11. Tell us about your target market: what are two or three frustrations or concerns that create a need for your services?

12. Discuss three or four things your client should prepare or do before for your first engaged client session.

13. Are there a few tasks or a checklist you advise every client (and non-client) to do?

14. What should a potential client ask you (or a peer professional)? What don't they know they ought to ask?

15. Tell us a client success story, others can learn from.

16. Do you have stories of how specific clients learned about you, perhaps through someone else, an organization, article?

17. Have you ever felt like saying "I told you so" to an (ex)client (lessons from "anti-success" stories)?

Blog Article Idea Section 3: Personal Articles Peel Back the Professional Lawyer and Help Reveal Who You Are (Remember, beyond your professional expertise, referrals and client interest are often due to your passions and personality.)

18. Why did you start your practice? Turning points in your career? Lessons you've learned and imparted.

19. Can you share any stories from your favorite pastimes, sports, hobbies, or family that can impart relevant lessons?

20. What distinguishes your peers (or competitors)— experience, certifications, other Bio/CV highlights?

21. Have you hired anyone new, or are about to? How has it increased your value or service to clients?

Blog Article Idea Section 4: My Favorite Type of Blog Articles—Those that are CROSS-PROMOTIONAL
(This gives you a number of ways to involve other colleagues, who you may often refer, be recommended by, or work alongside.)

22. Who can you interview to co-author with—referral sources, recommendations, relevant VIP?

23. Is a colleague presenting a seminar or organizing an event that would be relevant to your audience?

24. Are you doing anything with a charity or another organization?

25. Can you applaud your partner, staff, client or colleague?

26. Are there any relevant examples or metaphors from pop culture (movies, sports, politics, other celebrities)?

Oh, and a bonus trick of our trade: use Google Alerts. Login with your Google account to manage the keywords that you submit. Google will then send you article links that mention those terms. Remember to use esoteric jargon, or else you'll be inundated with very mundane articles. Also, you can use book titles, authors, and other VIP celebrities in your field.

What other ways do you use to think up blog articles (besides ripping off ideas from your peers)? Maybe you'll be the 27th idea in the next edition! We're looking forward to adding your idea (just make sure it's not already there). E-mail your ideas to vik@phoneBlogger.net.

Engage SEO and Readers with the *BLOG BLING 7*

Monotonous, long-winded blocks of writing are boring and cause the eyes to glaze over. We all prefer to skim and skip around articles, even if just to see if it's worth delving deeper. Thus, your blog articles ought to stand out and be eye-catchy. Moreover, such article structuring can even help improve your SEO ranking: professional Internet marketers like us can code your articles with tags (keywords), categories, and other metadata.

Bling out your articles with what I call "blog jewelry." (For those a tad bit old-school, "bling" is a slang term for jewelry or other ornamentation that purposely calls attention. It's like the "sound" light would make were it to "bling" off of something shiny.

Like jewelry, too much "blog bling" can distract and be gaudy. But used well, blog bling makes your articles:

- More attractive and eye-catchy

- Well-accentuated with important points

- More social media friendly

- More SEO friendly (Ask me how they can be coded to boost SEO.)

• More interactive with comments, forwards, and shares.

Here are 7 Jewels to Bling your Blog:

1a. Phrase-bolding helps to highlight specific points, which may otherwise be hidden within a paragraph

1b. *So does colored text, italics, indents, ampersands, dashes and other creative punctuation!*

2. Short paragraph, short words, and short sentences all keep text airy.

3. Numbers attract the eyes.

4. Sub-headings, numerical or bullet points, quotes, links, or pulled-out phrases.

5. Images: photos, diagrams, headshots—*worth a thousand words.*

6. Sign-off with a *blog signature*, like an e-mail signature. Ensure your contact info goes along for the ride when a reader prints the article, or if another website "scrapes" (steals or syndicates) your content.

7. Conclude with a *Comment Ask*— a blog article's call-to-action. The lamest call-to-action is offering a free consultation or "Call us if you have any questions." Instead, use calls-to-comment; ask readers to comment or to "do something" independent of a "free consultation."

Now that you're conscious of it, you'll see these tricks-of-the-trade in mainstream media and popular blogs. Keep these seven jewels in your mind to bling your own blog articles, social media, and e-mail newsletters. I look forward to seeing your good examples, and feel free to share gaudy examples of when blog bling went wild (vik@phoneBlogger.net).

12 Ways to Get Readers to Do Something

The whole point of blogging, being active on social media, and sending out newsletters is for your followers and subscribers to do something (for their benefit first, then yours). In marketing, we call this a "call-to-action." Many ads, presentations, and blog articles end with an impotent, "Call me if you have questions" or a lackluster "Call for a free consultation."

This is a wasted opportunity: after all, won't they call you when the time is right anyway? But what about before then, when it's not so urgent? Isn't there anything the reader can do now? What if the post, newsletter, presentation, or blog article isn't for the reader—but for a loved one or colleague of the reader?

The potential of the Internet is that it's an interactive network. At the very least, engaged readers ought to feel compelled to add a comment to your blog, to the LinkedIn Group, Facebook page, or Tweet. Every time someone interacts with you, it's one more way they are remembering you. And by nature of the social media platform, they are often tacitly sharing you with their contacts (like viral marketing).

To Help, I've Curated 12 Clever Alternatives Into What I Call *The Do-Something Dozen*:

1. End with something like, "Do me a favor . . ." and then ask for what you want, like general feedback.

2. Are there any time-sensitive tasks to be done or that will be due before a deadline? This is a call-to-action that readers will feel compelled to share with others.

3. Question the readers for their answers. This can lead to follow-up articles.

4. Ask for examples or frustration scenarios. This helps them relate to your points.

5. Offer a survey or poll (like #4 but with choices). Results of which can even be published.

6. Ask readers for their questions. Likewise, great for future articles.

7. Additions? "Am I missing anything?" No need to exhaust a topic; whet their appetite.

8. Critique and Disagreements? If done constructively, this can start a very informative and fulfilling discussion. Of course, beware of providing legal advice or information too specific.

9. Invite readers to an event that you're hosting, presenting or exhibiting at, or simply attending. This includes seminars, teleconferences, webinars, or relevant parties.

10. Offer a link to read the rest of the article, or download an e-book, audios, videos, etc. You can even capture e-mail addresses this way Download/Link Offer: Tools and Multimedia, past posts.

11. Ask the readers: "Can you share this article *with* . . . (a specific demographic: job title, age range, interests, etc.)" *or* "*when* . . . (a specific trigger moment: engagement, new hire, divorce, etc.)"

12. What's the first step or next step to implement what you're detailing in your article, before calling you? It's a great tip to get them started in the right direction.

These calls-to-action are not mutually exclusive. How can you use more than one in the same article? I look forward to seeing your examples. Share your posts with me: vik@phoneBlogger.net.

Leverage Your Time and Traffic by Co-Blogging: 6 Real-Life Examples

Blogging can brand you as an expert. Moreover, your blog can also help you leverage the reputation and recognition of others. Co-blogging includes co-authoring articles, guest blogging on someone's website, or swapping articles with another (for their blog, social media, and/or newsletter). By co-blogging, you leverage each other's time, topics and website traffic. **Here are three models (two examples each)** of how bloggers are exchanging new content for new contacts:

1. Cooperative Bloggers, like *Healthcare in Compliance* or *The Insurance Pro'*

When Ester Horowitz wanted to launch her blog, she had a vision of creating a resource for physicians, group practices, clinics, hospitals, and other healthcare businesses. They are under extreme scrutiny and compliance obligations. While Ester's expertise is in developing compliance management processes, she doesn't operate in a vacuum. As a professional, Ester often calls upon the expertise of other specialists. Why wouldn't she reflect that in her blog?

Instead of *Healthcare in Compliance* being a solo soapbox blog for her, Ester has created a platform for her colleagues. She asked some of her closest colleagues, who are also adept at writing, to participate; most of them have their own blogs. It's pretty easy for them to share excerpts, highlights, and other content with the cooperative blog. While she most regularly contributes, Ester also has a roster: they are not simply "guest bloggers," they are contributors. As their strategic relationships flourish, their blog can become a whole lot bigger than the sum of its posts.

Similar, but different, are the relationships between Jay Silverman, Seth Jonas, and Tomer Dicturel. They once belonged to a chapter of *Business Network International* (BNI) where their relationships and referrals grew. Jay wanted the benefits of a blog and social media marketing, without its burdens. He brought together two other complementary professionals to launch *The Insurance Pro's* blog.

Seth and Tomer are experts in their respective fields. All three of them now benefit by having a thriving blog, social media content to promote, and an e-mail newsletter that goes to each other's network of contacts. As an evolution of their networking experiences, their on-line networking can be even more efficient.

2. Co-authoring Bloggers, like Judy Heft or Mendy Lipsker

Simple testimonials are rather pedantic. Rather, stories of distress where a solution is uncovered is wrought with suspense, surprise and satisfaction. That is what Judy Heft achieved when she interviewed her friend Jane in her article, "Identity Theft: Falling Through The Cracks In A Foreign Land." This is an example of how to interview someone to bring out your point.

Likewise in a different way, Mendy Lipsker achieved his point. In his article, "8 Big Mortgage Mistakes and How to Avoid Them," Mendy invited Joseph Meerbaum, Esq., to guest blog. While guest blogging is an easy way to exchange content, it can easily seem out of place: a stranger in the home. Rather, Mendy went one step further: he introduced his colleague and made him (and readers) feel welcome. Mendy's experience running a networking group shows.

3. Aggregation by Associations, like *NYSCDM* or *Gotham Networking*

Aggregation by Associations is now trending: more and more membership groups are inviting its members to submit their blogs (and/or individual articles) to their cooperative blog. Everyone benefits: the association gets to have a thriving blog, and members benefit by showcasing their expertise, potentially marketing through the Association and learning from one another.

The *New York State Council on Divorce Mediation* (NYSCDM) has an open platform for its members to submit their blog articles. While the percentage of member participation is low, they have enough consistent bloggers to make their blog thrive. Those who do regularly contribute are able to benefit from increased exposure through their professional association. Most of them are leaders in their profession and benefit from their networking savvy.

On the other hand, Gotham Networking has a two-tier co-blogging platform:

1. Each day is assigned to a specific author. This way, Gotham is ensured a daily blog. Authors engage the membership through interesting content and through a friendly competition of who can get the most comments. Those who do comment benefit from the increased exposure (name recognition) within Gotham and throughout the Internet.

2. *Gotham Networking* recently launched a sophisticated online networking platform, rivaling LinkedIn. One of its homepage areas, called *Gotham Shares,* is a membership Wall (a la Facebook). While self-promotion is prohibited, members are encouraged to promote their blog articles. Like the daily blog, these posts are accessible by Gotham members and may be indexed by Internet search engines, like Google.

How Can You Follow These Examples?

I suggest launching a cooperative blog only with close colleagues, preferably with those you already have a working relationship (mutual clients or an on-going exchange of referrals). It will be essential to coordinate timetables and hold one another accountable. Thus, a strong relationship, and a leader, ought to be established.

Co-authoring articles can be a pain in the neck: going back and forth with revisions can drive you batty. If you do want to co-author an article, I suggest doing so on a system like Google Docs, where each of you can edit the same document (simultaneously if necessary). This will prevent "revision/attachment hell." I can't imagine running phoneBlogger.net without a co-editing tool like Google Docs.

Better yet, do what Judy did: interview a client or referral source. Ask colleagues to share their perspectives and use it as verbatim as possible. You can transcribe a telephone conversation, or ask your colleague to answer three to five questions by e-mail. With a little polish, a Q&A format is a quick way to mimic a co-authored article. In similar fashion, Mendy handed the mic over.

Better yet, he introduced his colleague and topic. This way, the guest blogger wasn't being treated like a stranger.

These "content exchange" examples aren't exhaustive. For example, while swapping contact lists is considered spamming, swapping articles in an e-mail newsletter has even greater benefit. Likewise, cross-promote blog articles with colleagues via social media.

These examples aren't mutually exclusive; they are powerful when combined. Networking groups and associations can showcase blog links, aggregate member articles, plus encourage interviews and co-authoring among its members (and their associates). Do you belong to a peer-development organization (e.g., Bar Association) or referral-networking group? They probably don't yet offer a cooperative blog, LinkedIn Group, or e-mail newsletter.

No need to wait. Why don't you suggest this new member benefit? They have examples to follow, and can also lead by example. Interested members (charter co-bloggers) can form a coordinating committee. I'd be happy to help guide such an initiative.

Please e-mail me your questions (vik@phoneBlogger.net) and offer more suggestions as comments. Together, everyone achieves more!

About Vikram Rajan

Vikram Rajan is an on-and off-line marketing specialist for attorneys. In November 2012, ViK was an opening presenter at the NYC Bar Association's Small Law Firm Symposium. He presents frequently on bLAWging, social media, & word-of-mouth marketing, notably at the Asian American Bar Association of New York, New York Women's Bar Association, Nassau County Bar Association, Academy of Professional Family Mediators, New York County Lawyers Association, and others. Vik is on the Esquire Coaching team.

Website: phoneblogger.net
Facebook: facebook.com/vikram
LinkedIn: linkedin.com/in/vikramrajan
Twitter: @vikramrajan

Part II

Stand Out from the Crowd—
Be a Better & More Productive Lawyer

Chapter 7
From Average to Excellence: Advanced Interpersonal and Counseling Skills to Stand Out in Your Legal Practice

by Mirna Hidalgo, Esq.

Q: Why don't sharks attack lawyers? A: Professional courtesy!

Like you, I am a lawyer. Lawyers' jokes make me furious; I find them offensive and unfair. Many of them depict us as greedy beings whose sole interests are money, prestige and power. Of course they don't do justice to the many lawyers who entered the profession with the vocation to serve their clients, with a passion for solving analytical challenges and strong ideals of justice.

Yet, perception is all, and there are statistics out there showing that there is a generalized low level of confidence in lawyers. Many of these prejudices are as old as the legal profession. Today some preconceptions are founded on unrealistic fantasies fed by TV series or propagated by people who have never been in touch with a real lawyer. Unfortunately, many are also fueled by clients' bad experiences. This has an impact on the way clients approach us: many clients will already be negatively influenced by the time they arrive to your office and it is your job to change this negative predisposition.

Dismissing these popular beliefs without assessing whether there may be elements of truth behind the reputation – however unfair—would give some reason to deduce we are an arrogant class of people. In this chapter, we are going to look at some of these beliefs and offer ways of changing these perceptions.

Being a successful lawyer depends on many factors. You wouldn't be in the market if you would not already excel at:

- Constantly keeping up with substantive and procedural developments

- Having a clinical eye to understand the facts, focus on detail, and build up a logical argumentation

- Evaluating risks accurately

- Being a good drafter

- Working autonomously

- Understanding hierarchical relationships if you work in a law firm or corporation.

The list does not stop there, these days your chances of survival also depend on:

- Being results-oriented without excessive deliberation

- Maximizing use of internet and technology

- Understanding business development

- Coordinating with other specialties

- Excelling at project and time management

- Applying competitive pricing

Many lawyers master these competences, and they still find it difficult to keep client loyalty and attract more clients. I believe this has to do with the way they think of themselves: most lawyers view the practice of law as a set of legal problems that must be solved, rather than as a vocation to serve people. The legal issue at stake is the center of their focus, the persons who are behind those problems are considered incidental.

Whether you are a solo practitioner, working in a law firm or acting as in-house counsel, you cannot ignore that behind every single case or consultation there is a person: a client, a manager, a boss, a counterparty or an authority to persuade. Obviously the legal analysis must be impeccable. Assuming you are competing with other lawyers who are equally capable at those hard skills, *it is your ability to focus on the interpersonal relationships that will make you stand out.*

Let's review a handful of unpleasant but popular beliefs about lawyers and see how we can change these perceptions.

Competitive Versus Collaborative Styles

Lawyers are often seen as aggressive. Law school assumes that lawyers will be (for most of their time) pleading in front of a judge. Reality is that unless we are trial lawyers, we won't be litigating often. You will be performing a variety of tasks that require human interaction, from delivering advice, strategic and operational transactional assistance, to assisting in settlement negotiations, lobbying and representation.

Most formal legal education does not teach how to resolve conflicts and negotiate without automatically resorting to an adversarial role. Let me ask you this question: if you had to choose a reputation, would you rather be recognized for your toughness or your ability to collaborate?

Try these ways of approaching interaction:

1. Don't assume that clients always want to enforce their rights to the maximum. Your client may be happier with less than 100 percent risk coverage. You may be pushing her to spend time and money for results she did not want in the first place.

2. Reflect on your own "conflict personality." Do you tend to compete? Or do you tend to give much importance to a harmonious relationship with everyone? If you are too competitive, you may be ruining the chances of a deal; if you are too cooperative you may be giving away too much. Understanding when to compete and when to cooperate is crucial. Knowing your natural approach to conflict is important, so you can adapt your own behavior to the circumstances. Managing the tension between competition and cooperation is an art you can consciously master. Here is some guidance:

- If the matter is urgent, there may be no time to spend building relationships and you may need to adopt a sharper style.

- Simple negotiations, which can be valued in monetary terms, may not require a lot of relationship effort (e.g., agreeing on a purchase price), whereas integrative and collaborative styles tend to be more effective in complex relationships (e.g., building trust for a long-term outsourcing transaction or assisting in family matters).

Becoming Effective Communicators

Q: What do you get when you cross the Godfather with a lawyer?
A: An offer you can't understand

No good lawyer is going to argue that wording is unimportant. But hiding behind complexity is deceitful. We owe it to our clients to be the translators of technical jargon and speak a language they understand.

Effective communication is also about active listening. Active listening is straightforward and yet quite hard for lawyers because we are trained to advocate. Try these tips:

- Make a conscious effort to understand the other's needs and beliefs.

- Don't interrupt or judge.

- Ask open questions to elicit information truly needed, not to intimidate.

- Use silence: a pause may encourage the person to keep talking or may be appropriate to defuse too strong emotions.

The Need to Coordinate With Other Lawyers

You are most certainly already confronted with the challenges of working across teams and geographic zones. You just can't afford to upset a client with delays or additional costs because of lack of internal coordination. Consider that:

- Clients are best served through a single point of contact and an effective backup system. Revise your procedures to build a seamless internal cuisine.

- Teamwork creates trust: invest time in good relationships with lawyers across practice areas. Clients who see you act as a good team will believe in your ability to be their partner. (See Chapter 15 for more information on building a team.)

The Effect of the Billing System on Client's Trust and Loyalty

Much has been said about the disadvantages of the hourly fee system. Times when clients could afford to pick up the phone without discussing costs are over. Today they will leave you if they sense your firm focuses on maximizing billable hours instead of providing value.

As a former corporate legal manager, I've hired outside counsel for large multinational projects. I've always had a preferred relationship with counsels who could help me achieve my goals in a cost-conscious manner. This is what set them apart and made me come back for larger and more complex engagements:

- They were ready to offer ways of doing things even more efficiently and cheaper than I had instructed.

- They spent time understanding my goals and constraints.

- They were generous with information and sources, and empowered me to avoid unnecessary reliance on their services.

- They anticipated requests and were constantly aware of cost and time pressure on my side.

It wasn't just the price. A transparent charging system and a cost-effective mindset create trust.

The Role of Emotions in the Legal Profession

Four surgeons were taking a break and discussing their work. The first said, "I think accountants are the easiest to operate on; you open them up and everything inside is numbered." The second said, "I think librarians are the easiest; you open them up and everything is in alphabetical order." The third said, "I like to operate on electricians; you open them up and everything is color-coded." The forth one said, "I like to operate on lawyers; they're heartless, spineless and gutless."

Lawyers are not heartless; we are trained to assess emotions in those circumstances where they count for the law (self-defense, intention, emotional suffering in determining damages, etc.). Yet, emotions play a role in every single interaction. It is not because you explain to the client the lawyer-client privilege rules that she will instantly feel you are trustworthy.

As a lawyer, dealing with emotions is delicate. You can't become so involved that you would miss facts or blur your analysis. This is tricky: if you focus purely on facts your client may not feel understood. On the other hand, too much empathy can compromise your objectivity.

There are ways of looking at things from the client's perspective without losing independence. Try building rapport by carefully paying attention to what the client expresses:

- Is she stressed? Put your client at ease by creating a comfortable environment at your office. If you are attending a difficult meeting together, meet her ahead of time to prepare.

- Is she worried about costs? Explain your fee system upfront and clearly.

- If it is a corporate client, does she feel embarrassed because she cannot solve the problem? Give her credit for identifying the issues.

- If you are advising a company, have you taken time to understand the corporate culture and see in what context your advice will be relied upon? The way you present it may increase management's support and compliance.

You still need to be assertive and clearly explain the options, risks and limitations that apply to our opinion. Understanding your client's motivation will simply make your advice more suited without losing independence of judgment.

From Lawyer to Top Counselor

It is well known that soft skills are the hardest to learn. A contract law course will not teach you how to deal with people. In fact, you will find more answers by looking into other disciplines like psychology, behavioral economics and neuroscience. You may wonder how practical it is for you to embark in such a study. The good news is that a great deal of counseling and negotiation skills can be learned by self-reflection and practice.

What concrete steps can you take to improve your interpersonal competences?

Learn About Cognitive Biases

The first step in developing emotional intelligence is self-awareness. It is natural to encounter some defensiveness and denial at first. Becoming aware of cognitive biases will increase your Emotional Quotient (EQ).

We are all subject to certain automatic reactions. Biases are distortions that pre-program the way we process information. They help us manage anxiety and filter information so that we are not overloaded. For example:

Self-deceptive overconfidence—we are programmed to survive. Fighting predators required extreme self-confidence, so we tend to think that we are smarter than others—i.e., we reject ideas from opponents simply because they originate from the other side.

Fundamental attribution error—we tend to attribute successes to our own competence, and failures to external circumstances.

Confirmation and assimilation biases—we seek out evidence that confirms our preexisting vision of ourselves, and avoid evidence that contradicts our own beliefs.

Are you aware of these biases? If you recognize their effect you may be able to anticipate and adapt your reactions.

Nonverbal Communication Speaks Volumes

Observe your client's nonverbal unstated messages: stay alert to signs of stress or anxiety such as tense or shaky hands and a frown facial expression. A higher voice pitch and an accelerated breathing rhythm are usually signs of anxiety.

Monitor your own communication style to avoid being perceived as threatening:

• Have you established a connection? Try sitting at the same side of the table. After all, a client is not coming to your office to be examined. (See also Chapter 9 for more information on connecting to clients.)

• Paraphrasing may be useful to show your understanding of what the other person is saying.

• Nonverbal details like a gentle smile, even in serious affairs, may help. It is precisely when dealing with a rival counterparty that you should use body language that invites people to communicate respectfully. You will still encounter rude people. Stay polite and there is a higher chance they will reciprocate.

Preparing for Negotiations

Litigation and arbitration are formal adversarial processes. The skills you use to argue a case in front of a judge are not the ones you will need when persuading clients.

Many factors can affect the results of a negotiation: your client's strategic position, the facts, timing, personalities, etc. But nothing has a greater impact than the level of your preparation.

Your role in a negotiation is crucial and goes beyond classical risk assessment and drafting. You should help your client structure her goals, objectives, strategy and tactics. This is what I recommend:

• Use your natural skepticism to ask questions and test the relationship's real nature. Enquire about future needs to make sure your solutions are durable and flexible.

• Make sure the clients' expectations are managed by explaining risks upfront. Keep the lines open to discuss changes.

- Once objectives and priorities have been agreed, define roles at the negotiation table and understand who has decisional authority.

- Agree on the negotiation process with the other side. It will save lots of misunderstandings.

- Focus on understanding the other side's story rather than arguing who is right.

- Finding the best negotiated solution requires curiosity and creativity. Allowing freedom to think creatively may be counterintuitive for lawyers. We are trained to look for risk rather than seeing solutions. Think freely and then perform a risk assessment, but don't deprive your client of new alternatives.

Boosting Personal Influence

Personal influence relates to perception of status, power, attitude and position. Using persuasion within an ethical framework can help you inspire others even without authority. At the same time, you'll be able to recognize and deal effectively with manipulation.

If you agree that human behavior is not always the result of purely rational activity, you will also see that being right on the law and wrong on the people will hinder your success. It was only when I realized how many doors opened through behavioral drives other than reason that I started to appreciate the power of personal impact. This is how you can boost your influence:

- Many human reactions are self-defensive or motivated by fear. Identifying those emotions in yourself, your client and the opposing party will make you a forerunner.

- A couple of clichés that work: first impressions count and small talk matters. It is not all about being clever; people follow optimistic and kind persons naturally.

- Think about things you have in common with other people and build upon similarities.

- Don't expect to be smarter than others—people feel and resent this—just be honest.

- As Maya Angelou said, "People will forget what you said or what you did, but they never forget the way you made them feel."

- Don't be afraid to show some vulnerability. People who seem "normal" are not less competent. Work with grit and accuracy on your legal analysis, but relate to others with authenticity.

- Learn from your mentors and spend time sharing and teaching others what you know. Get inspired and inspire.

Becoming a Lifetime Learner

Interpreting your own emotions and observing interactions and organizational dynamics will make you grow professionally. Real relationship skills are best built through experience. Here is a recap of habits that will help in this direction:

- Take notes—keep a journal noting your preparation and negotiation results. Encourage your team to conduct post-mortem conflict and negotiations assessments.

• Ask for feedback frequently—listen to your peers, superiors and team. Mentorship and coaching are also good ways of keeping you accountable to your personal growth.

• Reflect on these questions: do you put people at ease? Are you good at building and mending relationships? Are you able to adjust your own mood?

• There is extensive bibliography on negotiation theory. You may also take tests—many are available online—to determine your conflict resolution natural style. These tests are of course not comparable to a psychological assessment administered by an expert, but they are fun to do and get you thinking about your own behavior.

• Offer free meetings to your clients to talk about their priorities and share background that triggers legal awareness so that they know when to contact you.

• Organize at least a yearly satisfaction assessment session with your best clients, run through joint negotiations and agree on best practices.

• Create templates that help you and your clients identify must-have's and nice-to-have's, risks and alternatives before a negotiation.

If you approach clients from a counselor perspective, and not from an academic argumentative mindset, your sales will skyrocket. I have caught myself many times trying to impress clients with a display of know-how. It takes courage to be able to simplify and come back to what the client needs to know. There is always opportunity to showcase your technical skills. Clients don't come to us to admire our impressive capabilities, they come for results.

Legal counseling is a "people business." Being yourself and playing to your strengths will make you confident to set your ego aside and concentrate on delivering excellent service.

Don't reinforce the prejudices about lawyers. Prove them wrong and show that the top modern legal professionals are not just experts trained in the law. They are counselors and true leaders. They can do business using rigorous legal skills, the highest standards of professional ethics and above all, a deep understanding of their clients.

About Mirna Hidalgo, Esq.

Mirna is a lawyer with 20 years of experience as chief negotiator and manager of in-house and outside counsel teams. As head of legal strategy and international outside counsel retention, she understood what made professionals stand out. She is the founder of Wiser Gems, a firm that advises companies and individuals in interpersonal skills development. Mirna focuses on strategic negotiation and personal influence and coaches professionals in career advancement, stress and conflict management.

Website: WiserGems.com
Facebook: facebook.com/pages/Mirna-
Hidalgo/1417488525153613
LinkedIn: be.linkedin.com/pub/mirna-hidalgo/5/21b/1a9

Chapter 8
A Different Way to Lawyer
by Gila Lee Adato, Esq.

Perusing the table of contents of this book, or simply coming upon this chapter, you may be wondering what the phrase "a different way to lawyer" means. In a nutshell, it means different from the many stereotypes, clichés and lawyer jokes that are all too commonplace in our society. Whether you are a lawyer or not, you are likely familiar with these perceptions. There is the boring nose-to-the-grindstone workaholic, the ambulance chaser, the greedy, the rich, the unethical, and the pit bull. The list goes on. What all of the stereotypes seem to have in common is the portrayal of lawyers as unrelateable and almost inhuman.

The problems associated with being the type of lawyer that perpetuates these passé ideas are very real. There are well over one million licensed attorneys in the US today. With that many lawyers out there, if people see you as being unrelateable, untrustworthy, unethical, unorganized or just plain unappealing they will look for someone else to do business with. (See Chapter 2 on more tips to create a compelling brand that defies stereotypes.) It's just that simple. It was once thought that being a lawyer pretty much guaranteed a six-figure salary. The fact is that simply is not the case today. With all those lawyers to choose from (and the world getting smaller thanks to modern technology and the Internet), you simply have to lawyer in a different way in order to succeed, thrive and perhaps even to create fulfillment in your professional life.

Lawyering in a way that dispels the many clichés and allows you to bring your *entire, authentic self* into your work is what is meant by lawyering in a different way. As the world changes, the need and opportunity to create a different way to lawyer is very real. Not only is the world changing, people are changing along with it. Everywhere you look people are creating new roles in work and business, and as lawyers we have the chance to pioneer change as well. In my vision, the unhappy, unfulfilled lawyer can be a thing of the past replaced by lawyers who connect with people, nurture relationships and are proud of all they contribute. In this chapter, you will get some practical and real world ideas about how to create that different way to lawyer for yourself. Keep in mind that it is an evolving process, an individual journey. The ideas and concepts I share in this chapter have come from my real world experience—from my triumphs and my struggles.

I have been a licensed attorney for over 13 years and have traveled my own unique path personally and professionally. I have and continue to work at creating a professional experience that reflects all of me and allows me to go to bed at night feeling fulfilled and proud while thriving financially. It is as I said, an ever-evolving process of invention and reinvention—one that may take a great deal of time and soul searching.

By way of a bit more background on me, after graduating from law school, I joined a small real estate practice. I quickly realized that the traditional law firm setting wasn't for me and decided I wanted to go in-house. I was told over and over that for several reasons (including my lack of real-life legal work experience), it wouldn't happen for many years, at best. Despite all the naysayers I remained determined. I got a contract position at Goldman Sachs, otherwise known as a long-term temp position in a quasi-legal department. From there, I was able to land a position at a small Wall Street brokerage firm – a compliance role. It wasn't even a legal job. Frankly, at the time I didn't even know what compliance really meant. Somehow I knew this was an important step for me. I spent almost seven years at that company playing an integral part of its massive growth. When I joined, I was either the 12th or 13th employee. During my tenure, my role and responsibilities grew. While still in my twenties I became the Chief Legal Officer, the youngest and only female member of the senior management team. I built and ran the legal and compliance departments. I had a team of people working under me and the company grew to have offices nationwide and eventually overseas as well. There were private planes, expensive dinners, expense accounts and big bonuses. I was pinching myself every day, amazed at what I was a part of and what I had turned my little compliance role into.

Yet as the years passed, I became less and less satisfied with what I was doing. It just felt as though there was no heart in it and that something was missing for me. I constantly found myself yearning for more, for something different. After almost seven years, internal issues started to surface at the company. Eventually I left the firm, relieved and heart broken all at the same time. So much of my identity was wrapped up in my professional role and now I was unemployed. Burnt out, I decided to take some time off. A couple of months quickly turned into two years. In that time I started doing some amazing volunteer work: teaching success and life skills to underprivileged children, mothers and their daughters in battered women's shelters, kids on probation and teenage inmates at Rikers prison. I also took many self-development and personal transformation classes and became a personal coach. Personally, I was growing but my bank account was depleting. I went back to finance part-time, and kept up my "heart-centered work," as I lovingly refer to it.

It was during these next few years as I found myself living what felt like a double life, that I started consciously creating this different way to lawyer and searching for a way to meld my professional life with the passion I had for the volunteer and heart-centered personal transformation work I was doing.

Eventually, I began finding answers and started to see how I could do that for myself. I researched legal practice areas I had never previously considered – like special education law – and after dealing with my own struggles to have children (as I write this I am five months pregnant with my second girl), I realized that there was a practice area that could be very much right for me: Assisted Reproductive Technology (ART). I am now in the process of reinventing myself as an ART law practitioner.

Through the years, I have carefully examined the actions and behaviors that have been the most powerful, effective and transformative in my efforts to lawyer in a different way. Below are my top ten . . .

1. Take What Works for You—Put a Pin in What Doesn't

When you "put a pin in it" you save it for later. Don't simply dismiss all or even any of the information being presented to you at any given moment, whether it be this material or anything else, on first read or reaction. By applying this strategy, you can gain boundless amounts of knowledge and insight that you would otherwise miss. I invite and ask that you consider all the concepts in this chapter, and this entire book for that matter, with an open mind and spirit and take the ideas that work for you even if there are others that don't.

Don't simply "throw the baby out with the bath water," as the saying goes. If despite being presented with a concept that doesn't ring true for you, you are still able to "put a pin in it" and allow yourself to remain open, you will likely be able to create value for yourself. It is often that which we find uncomfortable or foreign to us that leads us to grow in a positive and productive direction of self-renewal. Personally, engaging in this practice has opened my eyes to many life-changing concepts. In fact, often one's initial resistance is a strong indicator that there is something very powerful to learn or consider. The resistance is often simply the ego fighting to remain comfortable and avoid change.

2. Stop Feeling You Must Know Everything and Have All the Answers

It's simply not true, and it's unrealistic. While it may be tempting to always give an answer in the moment someone seeks your counsel, there are many times when you won't have the answer for a variety of reasons. Perhaps it is not your area of expertise or you aren't being given enough information to make a determination. Regardless of the reason, if you don't have the answer, say so. You are free to explain why you do not believe you should give the answer in the moment, if you so choose. Keep in mind that especially as lawyers, providing the wrong information can be detrimental to the party asking the question as well as to you. After all, you can open yourself up to liability in the event you give bad information and the person acts on it.

I personally have numerous business relationships that have endured and grown through the years, some that have even blossomed into strong mutually supportive friendships, because of my willingness to openly tell people that I don't have the answer they are seeking in the moment. That said, if I had simply stopped there and failed to research the answer, the results would be very different.

3. Be Realistic About, and Manage Expectations

It's better to under promise and over deliver. In the event you are presented with a situation as discussed and you don't have the answer immediately, decide if you want to and are equipped to assist in the matter. If you will not assist, say so immediately. If you will, determine what you will need in order to move forward and how you will move forward. From there, keep the other party informed as you are progressing or even as you are coming up against roadblocks. Being open and remaining in communication will build confidence and trust. Even if you have no news, or do not have good news to share, reach out; do not go radio silent. You will be amazed at how much respect and trust you will glean from this simple action.

4. Make Every Effort to Get Your Ego Out of the Equation

Suggestions one, two, and three are all examples of ways in which we can set our ego aside. Each, however, was worthy of its own discussion. The ultimate result of setting our ego aside is that when we do so we rise above our problems. Yes, our problems will still be there, but our ability to deal with them is far better because we gain clarity and peace of mind by allowing ourselves some distance. We are better able to deal with whatever we encounter as we free ourselves from limited thinking and our attachment to being right or set in our ways and are able to be creative in our perspective.

5. Consistency is Key—Take Action No Matter How Tiny

You may have heard the saying "yard by yard life is hard, but inch by inch life is a cinch!" The saying couldn't be more true. As long as you remain in action and do so consistently, you will be amazed by the momentum that your actions create and the speed in which things get accomplished.

There has been a great deal written about how tiny actions can lead to big changes and results. Look for books and articles on the "Kaizen way" and the "ripple effect." It's inspiring and motivating to know that you don't need to take or make huge actions or changes all at once. Simply move forward and remain in action, even if the actions taken seem small. You will reach your goal before you know it.

6. Done is Better than Perfect

A huge mistake lawyers often make is allowing "analysis paralysis" to get the best of them and do nothing. So, in line with #4, take action and complete things. Check them off your list. If need be, you can often make changes later, but getting things done is essential.

7. Don't Believe or Feel You Must Talk "Big Talk," Talk a Lot, or Use Legalese or Other Jargon

Generally speaking, this will only create a disconnect and you will not convince anyone of your worth or abilities by doing so. People appreciate knowing and experiencing your humanness and will feel more comfortable with you and more confident in your abilities when you speak with them in a language they can understand and in a way that exhibits respect; you get what you give. If however, you are speaking to another lawyer or professional in your area of expertise, go ahead use the lingo. Bottom line—keep your audience in mind. It will go a long way.

8. If You've Nothing Smart to Say, Get the Other Person Talking

If you have nothing smart to say or anything of value to add during a conversation or meeting, the best thing you can do is get the other person talking, ideally about themselves. The other person will walk away thinking you are a genius and liking you tremendously. This was actually one of the first pieces of great advice I received when I began working on Wall Street and it was perhaps one of the most valuable that came my way. Following this simple rule can relieve a tremendous amount of pressure and save you from looking foolish. It allows you to listen far more carefully and hear so much more because your mind won't be busying itself with the need to come up with some smart remark. I can't stress enough how valuable this one piece of advice has been both professionally and personally.

9. Always Be Fair in Your Dealings

I don't know that this one needs much explanation as I think it is pretty much self-explanatory. I believe being fair will always benefit you, no matter how difficult it may be in the moment. I realize that often times it will feel as though doing so won't benefit you, but ultimately I have found that it always is best to do what you know to be the right thing. I have never regretted it but I have regretted those times where I wasn't courageous enough to do so. As the saying goes, "take the high road, it's less congested."

10. Stay Organized

Stay organized by finding a system that you can truly trust and that works for you. This is perhaps the most practical and tangible of all the concepts I have shared and it is incredibly powerful.

When we are organized and have a trusted system, we can relax knowing that nothing is falling through the cracks and that we are making wise choices and the best use of our time. There is so much technology available to assist you in these efforts; take full advantage. I'm not a fan of reinventing the wheel and I highly recommend a book which has its own cult following and has been a complete game-changer and life-saver for me. It's called, *Getting Things Done: The Art of Stress Free Productivity* by David Allen. Whether you fully implement Allen's system or use only a few of his tips I guarantee you this tool will be of tremendous value. There are many free resources available on his website as well. Google him and be amazed. (Also, see Chapter 10 for more organizing and productivity tips.)

With that, I wish you the best of luck in your many endeavors.

About Gila Lee Adato, Esq.

Gila Lee Adato, Esq., is a coach on the Esquire team. Gila practiced securities law for the majority of her career. Gila's unique and diverse experiences include having played an integral part in the building and growth of businesses, in and out of finance, as well as volunteering with mothers and their children in battered women's shelters and teenage inmates at Rikers prison, teaching them success and life skills.

Website: gilaadato.com
Facebook: facebook.com/GilaLeeAdatoEsq
Twitter: @GilaAdato

Chapter 9
Creating Meaningful Connections with Clients by Sharing Your Story
by Fred Schuldt

Being forced to survive three major intestinal surgeries and prostate cancer by age 40, I learned we can't do it alone. It's okay to ask for directions. It's okay to get advice. But when I decided to go on a journey to do more than just survive—a journey to thrive as a husband and father, youth athletic coach and personal financial advisor—I learned it takes connection. When you connect, people trust you. When you are trusted, you can have an impact on others, and when you have an impact on others, you can *thrive.*

Connection is the key to any strong relationship, especially an advice-based relationship, as with a coach an advisor or lawyer. Through sincere connection comes trust. And when there is trust, it's easier for people to make difficult decisions. Great advice is not only technically sound, but through a connection, it becomes much more. It becomes personalized and therefore more likely to be acted upon.

In order for clients to take action, they need to believe that your advice aligns with what they want to accomplish, who they are and their core values. To help people connect with you and actually take action on your advice, you first need to understand *them.* You need to understand what drives them. You need to know their story, their "Why." Deciding to take action may start with knowing the facts, but only when we have connected with someone on an emotional level can we help them tap into and understand the "why" that actually leads to action.

The challenge is that sharing a story from the heart means getting uncomfortable and being vulnerable. To really connect and be in a position to give great advice, you need to get others past their fears so their story can be revealed. As an advisor of any type (including being a lawyer), this begins with appropriately sharing not only your story, but also your "why." Being vulnerable gives others permission to do the same—to share, to open up, to discover and state their "why."

So, Why are Stories So Powerful?

Storytelling is in our DNA. For thousands of years we have told stories. Our greatest leaders have always been great storytellers. We have told stories to communicate new ideas and inspire change, to engage with others in order to educate and warn. We have told stories to celebrate success and, most importantly, to emotionally connect. If telling stories is in our DNA, listening is at our core. It's something we have always done; long before our ability to tell, we listened. Stories allow us to relax. When listening to a story, we don't need to do anything or make any decisions. And we tend to pay attention because we know that with a story something important might come along (e.g., a lesson, an insight, etc.). We remember stories long after we remember facts. Stories have the ability to stop the left brain from seeking more facts and allow the right brain to take the lead. The right brain is where we make the decisions to trust and take action. The right brain is where we emotionally connect. The power in sharing stories is the power to connect.

So, How Do You Share Your Story?

In order to share a story from the heart, you first must understand your "why." That takes digging down deep, and answering the question, "Why do I do what I do?" not just professionally, but also personally. Keep it simple. It needs to be from the heart and personal in order to emotionally connect, but you don't have a lot of time, and the meeting is not about you, it's about your client. Telling your story is not only an opportunity to connect, but to answer the key questions your clients are asking in their minds: Who is this person? How have they helped other people like me? Who do they represent? How can I take advantage of their expertise?

Even though some people are gifted storytellers, a good story doesn't just happen. Take time to craft your story, and practice it. Think about the questions your clients have about you, and answer those questions through your narrative. You need to be able to share the story about why you chose your profession. You need to be able to share the story about why you chose to represent the firm you're with or why you struck out on your own. You need to share what it is that makes you come alive and is most important to you. You need to share what you want your legacy to be. (See Chapter 1 for more information on how to live your intended legacy.)

When I meet a prospective client for the first time, I let them know that I am a financial advisor because I watched my Aunt Carol raise my four cousins on nothing but Social Security after her husband died without any life insurance. As a youth soccer coach, I communicate that I do not coach because I hope these kids will become professional players one day. I coach because I know the value of being connected to something special that is bigger than me, and I want to give kids the strength and courage needed to get up when adversity inevitably kicks them in the teeth. I also share that I'm Coach Fred, the motivational speaker, because I want to be a voice leading adaptive families through the struggle to move forward in spite of a changing reality.

After you have shared your story, tell your client or prospect that you did so because you want them to know it's okay to really share their story. Having created that connection, you can now listen, ask questions and seek to understand their "why." And yes, you'll need to give them the facts and explain what it is you'll do for them, but when you really know their story you can give them great advice—advice that they will actually take action on. When they take action on your advice, you'll have a greater impact. Consequently, you'll be more referable, and can then help even more people. Here's the great news: just as being vulnerable gives others permission to be vulnerable, when you THRIVE, you give people in your life the inspiration and permission to thrive as well.

When I went on my journey to do more than survive, I took great inspiration from the quote, "Don't ask what the world needs, find out what makes you come alive and do that, because what the world needs is more people that have come *alive*." But you see, this is not about solely and selfishly responding to the urge to satisfy our whims. I didn't leave my financial planning practice to become a full time ski bum, a fishing charter captain, or a professional soccer coach. Instead, I kept my financial planning practice and made time to do what I love with the people I love, to thrive, to connect, and to create stories that I can then share with my clients. I bring my passions into my professional life to help deepen my connection with my clients.

So, What Makes a Great Story?

If you researched this question, you'll discover many opinions about what makes a great story. For me, when it comes to creating your personal stories for sharing in a professional setting, there are four important factors:

1. It should be a story you *love* to tell.

2. The story should touch people's emotions in some way.

3. The story should create vivid images in the listener's mind.

4. It is the perfect story for your audience because it is relevant to them.

So, How Do You Craft Your Personal Story-Your "Why"?

Whether I'm crafting a 45-minute keynote speech or a story that I plan to share with my clients, I use a simple repeatable three-step process: Create-Share-Refine.

Step 1: Create—Schedule time in your calendar to work on your personal story. If you are like me, if it's in your calendar, then it happens! A time and place where you will have no distractions works best. Now when you are ready to begin, remember that more is less. The leader of the marketing division of the financial planning company I'm associated with shared an exercise where she has advisors think about sharing their story in six words or less. Earlier in this chapter, I shared my *why* using one sentence for each part of my story. I'm not saying you can only use six words or one sentence, I'm just reminding you to keep it simple and from the heart. Only give necessary details! Too many details can get "heavy" for the client to carry and they will be disappointed to hear so many details for no reason. Get inspired by experiences and people that have greatly impacted your life. Find a way to creatively share the following ideas:

- Who you are at the core. This could be a phrase, favorite quote or saying.

• Why you do what you do personally? What are your passions and what makes you come alive?

• Why you do what you do professionally? Why did you choose you area of expertise and your firm?

• A client example. This should be easier. It should include what the client's challenges were, what process you used to help them overcome those challenges, what the positive resolution was, and how that made an impact on you and your client.

Now, put it all together so you can move on to the next step!

Step 2: Share your story—Remember, it takes practice. You may want to start by practicing in the mirror or with those whom you trust. The more you share the story, the better it will be.

Step 3: Refine and repeat—See what works and what doesn't feel right. Try new stories so you can keep it fresh and add stories over time. When you are thriving and having an impact there will always be new stories!

When you share your stories, not only will you help a greater number of people and build a more successful practice, you will be happier. Sharing our stories allows us to take what we love, what makes us come alive, and not only use it to become more successful at what we do, but also be more connected and fulfilled in our lives.

There is huge power that comes from sharing our stories. Are you ready to really share yours?

About Fred Schultz

Fred was already considered by some to be an inspirational leader and gifted storyteller . . . traits that came in handy during his seemingly normal life as a loving family man, successful executive, and coach. But it took the impending loss of that life to truly forge these talents — giving them purpose while giving their bearer perspective. His mission is to arm those around him with the personal skills and inner strength to face adversity before it strikes.

Website: Coach-Fred.com
Facebook: facebook.com/meetcoachfred

Chapter 10
Maximize Productivity:
Tips for Organizing Your Office
by Amy Neiman

"For every minute spent in organizing, an hour is earned."
— Benjamin Franklin

Reflect on the above quote. What would you do with an extra hour of time?

Consider the following, the *Wall Street Journal* found the average U.S. executive spends one hour per day searching for misplaced information as a result of messy desks and disorganized files. This adds up to six weeks per year searching for needed paperwork.

It can be frustrating to constantly be searching for files and items you need in your office. It makes sense to take time now to save time later. By organizing and implementing a solution that works for you, you can improve your productivity.

An organized home and office means less clutter and adds more time to your day. Finding "homes" for your belongings increases your ability to find what you need when you need it. Being organized is more efficient and increases your health and happiness, which translates to less stress.

Being organized impacts your work habits and environment as well. Increased productivity means increased profits. Less time in the office also means you have more time to spend with family and friends.

Where to Begin?

Improving productivity is all about strategies and processes. Once you adhere to some basic strategies and implement processes to certain phases of your work, your productivity will improve and your business can begin to work on its own.

Not all strategies and processes work for everyone. Experiment to see which strategies and processes work best for you. When you find something that works, stick to it.

Strategies You Can Implement This Week

Consider strategies as supportive partners in your quest for achieving success in your professional and personal life. Some of the following strategies may sound really simple, but without adhering to them, you will not achieve your goals.

Make Yourself a Priority

Start with you. Taking care of yourself mentally and physically should be a priority. If you're not getting enough sleep, then you won't be able to be present and effective for your clients. Take steps to maintain your health.

According to a *Nielsen Survey for University of Bristol, 2010,* "Three-quarters of surveyed employees saw an improvement in their time management when they exercised before work or at lunchtime."

Some suggestions for making your health a priority include:

• Schedule a workout in your calendar just as you would a work appointment.

- Be consistent with your regimen.

- Exercise with a friend so you are accountable and less likely to skip an exercise session.

- Hire a personal trainer to help you establish a routine that works for you.

- Take a walk during lunch.

- Meditate, get a massage, dance, or take a Yoga class.

After your exercise routine is established, you'll notice an increase in time management productivity during the day. One of the best things you can do for organizing your life is make yourself and your health a priority.

Manage Your Distractions More Effectively

Distractions break your level of concentration, which greatly decreases your productivity during the day. A study in *Fast Company Magazine* found it takes a person an "average of 23 minutes and 15 seconds to get back to the task" after an interruption.

To help curb these interruptions and decrease the number of distractions you have during your day, strive to include the following:

- Set aside one hour of undisturbed time each day to focus on important tasks.

- Group similar tasks together; for example, spend a block of time returning calls, running errands, or scheduling meetings.

- Most importantly, limit checking e-mails to certain times during the day.

- Keep the top of your desk cleared of any distractions such as unnecessary files, trinkets, books, bills, etc.

Take 15 minutes at the end of your day to clear your desk and put away any items no longer needed.

Set Professional and Personal Boundaries

This strategy is one of the more difficult ones to implement. To be successful, one needs to establish specific work start and stop times. It is easy to get sucked into working longer hours and bypassing any boundaries you may have set for yourself. Not respecting your boundaries makes you less effective. In addition, your health may be negatively affected by the additional stress from working longer hours.

If you work from a home office, then it is imperative that boundaries are set and communicated to your family. Have a sign on your door signifying when you're working or establish a time schedule and ask your family to respect it. Consistency is the key to success in the home office.

Another suggestion is to schedule personal and professional events using the same calendar so all your appointments are in one place. This limits the chances of double booking. Don't forget to include travel times in the block scheduled.

As mentioned above, test out different strategies and see what works best for you and your work style.

Now that you have some general rules set up for getting organized and being more productive, let's shift to the processes that will make your life easier overall.

Organizing Your Files

The one area that needs the most organization in any business is your files and filing system. It is important you create a folder and color-coded filing system. Categorize your file folders into four types:

1. **Active and Important**—These are active cases, so this information should live on your desk in a cascading file holder.

2. **Ongoing Cases**—These are cases in progress that do not require immediate attention. They should be stored in your desk drawer so they are easily accessible when needed, but don't take up precious real estate on your desktop.

3. **Closed Cases**—These files are closed cases and may only be needed for reference or on an archive basis. File them away in a filing cabinet behind your desk, or in a location outside your office.

4. **Deep Storage Archive**—These files are sent to another room or an offsite facility, as they are not current.

Use a color-coded system not only for your general use, but for your client folders as well. It is important not to use more than five colors. For example, a client who is a matrimonial lawyer uses the following system to identify what types of cases each file represents: blue for prenuptial agreements, green for divorce cases, red for custody cases, orange for estate planning, yellow for general use. An investment lawyer could code his files such as, U.S. projects in blue, Europe/Asia in green, Fund to Funds/Real Estate in yellow, Mutual Funds in red, and general use in orange.

Use the system that best works for your files. Another idea is to use the color folders for types of motions.

It is a good idea to add color to your general folders and labels. For folders with important information, color-code them so they stand out; for example, red equals urgent information, yellow is action items, etc. Add as many folders as you need to help find important papers quickly. Have these folders close at hand:

- Action: urgent

- Action: non-urgent

- Research

- Bills to pay

- Follow-up calls

- Follow-up prospects

Label, Label, Label

Physically labeling items, drawers, and folders is the best way to declutter your office. The more you label in your office, the easier it will be to find items you need.

Don't forget to designate the corresponding number on each label based on where it is in the workflow process. This will help to move files accordingly so they can be filed in their correct storage place and help when you have office staff locate a file in need.

To ensure both online and offline filing systems are in-sync, all of your computer files and e-mails should be labeled the same as your paper folders. Utilizing the same system and the same file-labeling scheme will enable you to easily find the folders both digitally and via hard copy.

If you want to alphabetize your folders in your e-mail or on your computer, then use an underscore in the beginning of a computer folder name to get them to come up to the top of the list. As soon as a document comes into your inbox act on it and then file it right away into the respective folder.

To-Do Lists Really Work

A to-do list is the best option to stay focused during the day. You can create your to-do list for the next day either before you go to bed or first thing in the morning.

Make sure you have a reliable system to record your list. A suggestion would be to use a notebook. This way you always know the notes are in the same place. There are now many different mobile applications that can help you as well; such as Evernote, Remember the Milk, and Asana.

Not only will your list keep you focused on what tasks need to be completed and tackled, it also will give you satisfaction when you check off each item after it is finished. To-do lists are another process that helps to keep your work organized and you on task.

Multi-Tasking is Overrated! Focus On One Task at a Time

Multi-tasking is easier these days yet it is not always efficient. When working, focus your energy and time on one task until it is completed. It's much easier to finish and deliver results on one project, than to start multiple projects and not finish any. The one task at a time method maximizes productivity and concentration and helps you to achieve your goals faster.

A study in the *Journal of Experimental Psychology* found people who multi-task are less efficient than those who focus on one project at a time (Star-Telegram 3/1/2003, *Study in the Journal of Experimental Psychology*, Ann McKinney). In addition, time lost switching among tasks actually increases with the complexity of the tasks. Using the same tips recommended above to manage interruptions and distractions would be helpful.

When possible, eliminate multi-tasking and focus on one task at a time to increase your productivity.

Timers Help Keep you Focused and on Task

Timers can help with completing important tasks by keeping you on track. A timer is equally helpful when doing online research or checking e-mail as it limits the time spent on these items and helps to avoid further distractions.

A recommendation is using the Pomodoro application on your computer or Smartphone for 25 minutes while you read and respond to e-mail. It includes a short five to ten minute break to keep you focused. This is great, as we all know how distracting the Internet can be.

Timers can also help you to meet project and everyday demands. For instance, if you're feeling overwhelmed or don't know where to start, set a timer to force you into action. Once the time starts, you'll have no choice but to choose a task and get started. Timers really help to keep you on pace and focused as they create mini-competition scenarios.

Delegate to Your Support Team

Adding a support team to your practice enables you to delegate the less involved tasks so you can focus your energy on moneymaking activities. This may involve a cost; however, you can use the time saved to make more money by freeing up your time for more important tasks.

Sometimes there are tasks you don't like to handle such as social media, blogging, and website design. If this is time consuming, then hire a professional who works in these areas of expertise daily to help you. Here are some examples of areas to delegate:

- Bookkeeping

- Filing

- Technology "issues" as social media

- Website design

- Answering phones

- Cleaning home or office

- Running errands

- Scheduling meetings

A Virtual Assistant (aka VA) handles a large array of activities, including many on the above list. When retaining the services of a VA, the most important part is that you interview and select the right person for you. If you need blog specific help, then it's best to hire someone who only handles blogs, rather than bookkeeping.

Before the interview, sit down and make a list of all the desired qualities you would like to find in a VA. Then use this list during your meeting to determine if she/he will be a good fit. Be selective; intuition is there for a reason. (For more tips on selecting your dream team, see Chapter 14.)

If you have retained someone and they aren't working out, take action, and make a change. Don't wait. Keeping someone onboard who isn't productive won't help your progress.

Once you've retained someone and have trained them on processes specific to your practice, you can focus on more important tasks. At this point, a huge weight will have been lifted off your shoulders and you may feel freer and lighter in some respects. This is a positive step, as it will open you up to being more creative and productive.

Two More Tips

If you have an assistant or a support team onsite, create an inbox for each person. Every day, each support person should check his or her inbox to handle whatever items you have placed in the box. To ensure the proper action is taken, use post-it notes or a customized assignment sheet or checklist to communicate what actions are needed.

Another tip for delegation is to have your VA or assistant file all of the business cards you have collected. Either ask him or her to enter the information into a Customer Relationship Management software system (CRM) or have your VA create a binder and filing system.

The easiest and least expensive way to file business cards is to use a three ring binder. Purchase the business card holder page inserts to store the cards and a set of alphabetical divider pages. Once you've delegated this task, you will have eliminated some of the clutter from your desk. Plus, these cards will now be easily found in the future. If you want to rid yourself of business card clutter altogether, use a mobile application such as Card Much or CamCard, which captures the content in the card digitally.

The Most Effective Organizing Tip—The Fast 15!

The key to this tip is to take 15 minutes at the end of each day to organize your desk and workload for tomorrow. It sounds so simple, yet it is really effective at setting you up for success the next morning. Here are the steps you need to take:

- Review your calendar for tomorrow noting any big deadlines and meetings.

- Add important tasks into your schedule as appointments to be completed.

- File the folders and papers you no longer need that are on your desk.

- Take out folders and information needed for the next day so you are prepared when you arrive in your office.

- Clear your desk and put away any office supplies or items used during the day so your desk is a clean slate for tomorrow.

- In addition, you can do The Fast 15 at home before retiring to bed. To do this, follow these steps:

- Straighten areas by gathering belongings and placing them in their designated "home."

- Neaten up as necessary to eliminate clutter in the frequently used rooms.

- Review your family's calendar and look to see what important appointments or activities are happening tomorrow.

• Prepare items for the next day and put them together in one place so they are easily retrieved on the way out the door.

• Prior to getting into bed, put together your outfit that you'll wear the next day.

Final Thoughts

Organizing your office is the best way to increase your productivity. The strategies and processes noted above will help you take the necessary steps to getting your office organized as quickly as possible. Take time every day to eliminate clutter and get organized.

In addition to hiring a VA or a support team, Professional Organizers are also a great resource. If you're feeling overwhelmed with this process and are not sure where to start, call a professional organizer to help you. They will help you set up systems that make the most sense to you, and can be maintained for the long run. Take the task of organizing, filing, and setting up processes off your plate so you can focus on other important tasks.

Once you get organized, you will maximize productivity, increase revenues, reduce stress, enhance happiness, and improve your quality of life.

About Amy Neiman

Amy Neiman is the founder and CEO of A Simplified Life, LLC. She combines a passion for an organized space and the love of problem solving, with energy and motivation to achieve goals. She is a member of the National Association of Professional Organizers (NAPO), and active in the local New York Chapter (NAPO-NY). She adheres to their Code of Ethics. She's also a member of the National Association of Professional Women (NAPW).

Website: AmyNeiman.com
LinkedIn: linkedin.com/in/amyneiman
Twitter: @amy_neiman

Chapter 11
SASS-E Time Management System for Lawyers

by Ann Jenrette-Thomas, Esq., CPCC

A lawyer's ability to manage time directly affects the standard and quantity of his or her legal work, the quality of service provided to clients, job satisfaction, and your personal life. There are 168 hours in a week. If you worked 60 hours each week (let's face it—we're lawyers, and there is no 40-hour work week for most of us!) and slept eight hours every night, you would still have 52 hours left in the week. The question is what will you do with your 52 hours? 52 hours is more than enough to make time for all the things that matter most within each week.

Contrary to popular belief, time management is not about managing time – it's about managing your *priorities*! The *SASS-E Time Management System* is designed to help you identify and manage your priorities (thus, your time). SASS-E is an acronym that stands for the following:

S= Strategize
A= Adopt a Productivity Mindset
S=Systematize
S=Set Aside Time for Self-Care
E= Eliminate Time Wasters

I'll go over each of these factors in detail below.

Strategize

In order to make the best use of your time, you must set clear goals for what you want to accomplish. Goals cannot be created in a vacuum. They are intended to move you toward the ideal life you want to create for yourself and the things that matter most to you—i.e., your priorities. As a preliminary matter, identify the overall impact or result you want to have in each of the following areas of your life:

- Career/Business

- Significant Other

- Family (e.g., children, parents, extended relatives)

- Health

- Home

- Finances

- Spiritual/Personal

- Friendships

- Other (specify)

Now, as challenging as this might be, rank each item in order of priority to you (there is no right or wrong answer; this is completely subjective). From this set of priorities, we will begin to set goals.

In order to accomplish your goals, you need to understand what they are. Goals are effective and more likely to be accomplished when they are SMARRT:

S—Specific: The goal has to be concrete. (e.g., stating, "I will bill two extra hours this week" is more specific than stating "I will bill more.")

M—Measurable: It should be easy for anyone to tell that you've accomplished it because you can measure the difference between where you currently are, and where you will be when the goal is achieved. Using the previous example, you can easily determine whether you have in fact billed two extra hours this week.

A—Achievable: You have the ability (skills, qualities, resources, time, etc.) to accomplish the goal. Your achieving the goal is not contingent upon factors outside of your control.

R—Realistic: Given your abilities, other goals, priorities and resources, it's reasonable to assume you can achieve the goal as stated.

R—Resonant: Achieving the goal will bring you fulfillment and is in alignment with your overall priorities. An example of a goal that is not resonant is doing something simply because you feel you have to or because other people want you to, but you have no genuine interest in the outcome. Note, in an effort to accomplish your goals, you may from time to time have to engage in tasks that you don't feel thrilled about doing, but are still important to accomplishing the overall goal (e.g., most law firm attorneys do not enjoy keeping track of their billable hours, yet it is essential to building business or, in the case of an Associate, making partner). People are more likely to achieve goals that they are excited about.

T—Time-Bound: It has a deadline. Reviewing your list of priorities from above, develop a list of three to five major goals you want to accomplish over the next year. These goals should move you closer to the overall impact you want to have in the top priority areas of your life. (Note: you will not necessarily have goals that will help you address each priority area within a year. The impact you want to have in each priority area will be met over the course of a lifetime.) Write out each goal using the SMARRT goal system.

Next, divide each annual SMARRT goal into key milestones that must be accomplished every quarter (90 days), and set loose deadlines by which each milestone should be accomplished. These milestones will progressively move you toward achieving your annual goal in a timely fashion. Take the 90-day milestones a step further and break it down into milestones that would need to be accomplished on a monthly basis (30-day milestones).

Adopt a Productivity Mindset

Once you've created your annual SMARRT goals, and 90-day and 30-day milestones, it's important to develop a productivity mindset. A mindset means a fixed mental attitude or disposition that predetermines a person's responses to and interpretations of situations. Adopting a productivity mindset means that you develop a fixed mental attitude of using your time, energy, and resources in a manner that allow you to meet your SMARRT goals.

To adopt a productivity mindset, first get clear on *why* accomplishing each goal is important to you. Consider what you would gain by accomplishing the goal. For example, if one of your goals is to lose 15 pounds, perhaps the reason why that goal is important to you is because you want to have more energy and reduce your risk of getting heart disease—essential elements to have a long career. Remind yourself of your "why" frequently. By doing so, you can foster a productivity mindset.

Another way to develop and maintain a productivity mindset is to use the technique of visualization. Visualization is a technique where, in your imagination, you see yourself achieving your desired result. The more vivid the image is, and the more senses involved in the visualization, the more it can motivate you. This technique is used by elite athletes, corporate executives, and successful entrepreneurs. There are two ways in which you can use the visualization strategy: (1) visualize yourself accomplishing your SMARRT goal; and (2) visualize the successes you will accomplish in any given day.

A third method to adopt and maintain a productivity mindset is to use affirmations. An affirmation is a form of auto-suggestion, in which a statement of a desirable intention or condition is deliberately repeated in order to reinforce it in the mind. Neurons connect in your brain by attaching to thoughts. Thoughts then become organized into a pattern. Affirmations can interrupt unproductive patterns (e.g., those that lead to procrastination). Affirmations, when practiced deliberately and regularly, start breaking the long-term relationship your nerve cells have with your negative or unproductive thoughts, and re-wire them to your new, affirming beliefs. Examples of productivity affirmations include, "I am a productive, motivated and highly-driven person," or "I am productive even during tough or boring projects."

Systematize

In order to manage time effectively so that you meet your goals, you have to develop systems that will ensure your success. Here are some systems that can help you manage your time (See Chapter 10 for additional productivity systems):

Create a Master Calendar

One mistake many lawyers make is keeping their personal and work activities in separate calendars. Instead, have one calendar where both your personal and work commitments are included. Block out all appointments that are pre-scheduled (meetings, doctor visits, etc.). For each scheduled activity, also block out any relevant prep time (e.g., commuting, getting dressed for work, etc.).

Think about things that you have to do on a regular basis (e.g., weekly planning time, tracking billable hours, laundry, grocery shopping, house cleaning, checking e-mail, etc.). Calculate the average amount of time these things take and then create a *regular* time slot for them (e.g., Saturday from 9:00 a.m. to 11:00 a.m. is laundry time).

Weekly Planning Time

Each week, set aside 30-60 minutes to plan the following week, using a week-at-a-glance system (on paper or virtual). Review your 30-day milestones and see what must be accomplished during the week to advance those milestones. Each week, think about what you will do to take care of your mind, body, and spirit.

In addition, consider which relationships in your personal and professional life you would like to develop during the week. Make sure to plan *fun* time as well (dates, time with friends and family, alone time, etc.). These will help manage stress and ensure you have a clear head to focus on work.

Develop a Master "To-Do" List

Keep two "To-Do" lists. One is a *Master To-Do List* that includes everything. Any and all tasks should be added to this Master List. Put deadlines next to these items and in parenthesis, note the estimated time it will take to complete each item. For large projects, break the tasks down into smaller chunks, each of which should take no more than two hours. This list should be easily accessible from all of your devices.

Develop a Daily "To-Do" List

Although I call this a *Daily To-Do List,* you will first implement this system during your weekly planning time. This helps you to keep track of the big picture of all the things you need to get done during the week. However, each morning or the night before, you should take 15 minutes to revise/update the list as necessary and plug it into your master calendar.

Pull items from your *Master To-Do List* and add to your Daily List. Code each item using an **ABC** system:

> "**A**" for things that must get done today (e.g., deadline is approaching).

> "**B**" for items that can be done within the next few days, but you would like to get them started today.

> "**C**" for items that can be delegated or deleted.

Quickly decide how you can get rid of the "C" items (e.g., for work items, ask an assistant, junior attorney, paralegal, or an intern to do them; for personal items, delegate them to another family member or outsource help). Prioritize each A&B item with a 1-2-3 system. Then, based on the estimated time to complete each item, start plugging them into your schedule, and tackle each one *in the order of its priority.*

Schedule Time

Designate time in your calendar to accomplish your tasks. Group like activities together. Make sure you schedule time each day for breaks, and add at least 30-60 minutes of "free" time to handle miscellaneous items (e.g., items that took longer than expected, client or colleague interruptions, impromptu meetings, etc.). I strongly recommend scheduling times to check e-mail, return calls, and work on social media—otherwise these things will interrupt your whole day! Note: You can plan to check e-mail for ten minutes every hour if you are concerned about ensuring a timely response to your clients or colleagues.

It's also important to schedule at least one hour of "uninterrupted time" each day where you can have focused attention on client or business development matters. During this time, keep your door closed, set your phone to go to voicemail automatically, silence your mobile devices, and close your e-mail.

Use a Timer

Use a timer to help you stay on track. Stick to the scheduled times as best as possible. If you're not close to finishing ten minutes before the time is scheduled to end, then estimate how much time it would take to complete the project, and find the next available slot (it may be on another day). Be willing to rearrange your schedule to accommodate time-sensitive materials, if necessary.

The first few weeks you implement this system takes a bit longer (about 60-90 minutes for weekly schedule, and 20-30 minutes for daily schedule), but then it gets easier and faster as you get the hang of it. Over time, you'll better judge how long things take you to do.

Although this system may seem rigid, it will ultimately give you the freedom and flexibility you're looking for. Plus, you'll feel great accomplishing all the things that matter most to you.

Set Aside Time for Self-Care

As a busy attorney trying to keep up with the demands of work and life, it can be easy to forget to take care of yourself. Self-care is an essential component of success. Regularly engaging in activities that help you take care of yourself allows you to have increased stamina and clarity. Regular self-care also increases self-esteem, self-confidence, and self-image—all of which enable you to take bolder actions.

One way to ensure that you take time for yourself in the midst of your hectic schedule is to create a daily ritual. Most of us start our days in a frenzied rush. We wake up, dash out of bed, jump in the shower and immediately start thinking about all the things we need to do, then we quickly grab a cup of coffee or tea and something to eat (if we're lucky), and rush to work. Think about the impact this morning routine has on your day. You might find that you are irritable, less patient, or frequently exhausted. In addition, you might find it difficult to concentrate. If so, create a daily ritual and observe the positive impact it has on your life.

A daily ritual is a ritual of self-care that you commit to doing each morning. The intent is to help you start your day right, feeling more grounded. The ritual can be as simple or as elaborate as you desire. If you are limited on time, incorporate a self-care ritual into what you already do. For example, say affirmations or visualize a productive day while you shower, or think of ten things you are grateful for as you commute. When you have additional time, create a more elaborate ritual, such as meditating, writing in your journal, or doing a longer exercise routine. There's no end to the creative things you can do to start the morning with rejuvenating self-care.

Having a daily ritual has a number of benefits. You will feel refreshed and ready to face the day. You will be better equipped to withstand your daily stresses with ease. Most importantly, it helps you maintain a more positive outlook.

Eliminate Time Wasters

In order to *manage* your time, determine where you are *wasting* your time, and change those behaviors. You can tell you're engaging in a time waster if the time you spend on the item does not yield a sufficient result. Common areas where people waste time are: focusing on items that are not urgent or important; failing to delegate tasks that don't utilize their strengths; checking e-mail or social media all day; and spending too much time on the Internet.

Use the following chart to help you identify where you are wasting your time, the impact it has on you (productivity, energy, etc.), and what could be a more productive use of your time instead.

Time Waster	What's It Costing Me?	What Can I Do Instead?

As you can see, the *SASS-E Time Management System* is more than just managing your time. It's a system that is designed to help you make the best use of your time in the furtherance of your true priorities. By having a strategy for accomplishing your important goals, adopting a productivity mindset, developing systems to implement your goals, engaging in self-care, and eliminating time wasters, you are bound to be more productive and fulfilled. Be patient with yourself. If you've struggled with managing your time, then implement the information provided in this chapter one piece at a time. If you fall "off the wagon," simply recommit and engage in the positive behaviors note.

"There are far too many people that waste their time telling themselves that they don't have enough time."
— Daniel Willey

About Ann Jenrette-Thomas, Esq., CPCC

Ann Jenrette-Thomas, Esq., CPCC, founder of Esquire Coaching, is an attorney, certified coach, and author. Ann has spent nearly 18 years helping business owners overcome obstacles to success. Ann calls upon the breadth of her experience, coupled with her extensive training and knowledge in organizational development and coaching, to provide her clients with effective solutions that balance both the viability needs of the business, and individual needs of the business owner to feel balanced.

Website: EsquireCoaching.com
Facebook: facebook.com/EsquireCoaching
LinkedIn: linkedin.com/in/annjenrettethomas
Twitter: @esquirecoaching

Part III

Special Strategies for Law Firm Partners

Chapter 12
Mastering the Mental Side
of Building a Solo Law Practice
by Tracy Dacko

As a lawyer trying to build your own business, you may be told that your worst enemy is your competition, the government, the economy or maybe even your accountant, but I'm here to tell you that your worst enemy is, in fact, you.

Your ego, your inner dialogue and your beliefs have the potential to do more damage to your business than anything or anyone else. (Uplifting, right? It's always nice to hear that you will likely sabotage your own business at some point.)

The good news is that when you are aware of what will potentially hold you back, and know the warning signs, it's much easier to change course before its too late. Let's start with your selfish evil twin: your ego.

Tackling Your Worst Enemy

When we hear someone referred to as "egotistical," we think of bold, outwardly arrogant characters like Gordon Gekko from the movie *Wall Street,* who steamroll weaker people for breakfast. While you probably don't fall into that profile, you still have egotistical urges, just like everyone else. Ego is the selfish part of you who always wants to win, be looked up to and be right. While it may not be a predominant part of your personality, it is always present to some degree. You can't escape it, but you CAN recognize it, call it out and keep it on a leash.

Ego can fuel your actions in ways that are counterproductive. It can stop you from seeing the truth, asking for help or making the right decisions . . . not to mention making you look inexperienced, insecure and insincere.

Ego Creates False Expectations

Many first time business owners prefer to focus on the *ego boosters* – like seeing the title "Partner" on your business card or having your name on the door – rather than the inevitable *ego busters* – like having to bring in 100 percent of the business yourself and realizing you suck at selling. Your ego has a tendency to dwell on these romantic expectations, about how easy it is to build business, that are not based in reality. Follow your ego and you're setting yourself up for disaster.

While you may be the best attorney out there, building a law practice – or any business for that matter – will expose you to tasks and competencies that have never even entered your mind, let alone come across your desk. And yes, your ego will think some of them are "beneath you." Partners at larger firms have assistants, computer tech support and a marketing department supporting their business development efforts, but as a solo, you ARE all of those things wrapped up into one overwhelmed individual. Being at the top of your organization *and* the bottom can be a tough adjustment for your ego. When you set your ego aside and move forward with realistic expectations, you'll find that you are better prepared to adapt to this new role of *Chief Everything Officer.*

Ego Creates Misguided Attachments

Your ego is great at clinging on to the things that YOU create – an idea, a belief, a product or your firm as a whole. It gets attached. Your ego falls in love with this thing you have created together.

The danger is that we all know love can be blind. This attachment your ego creates is by no means objective and it can cause you to miss inherent faults or omissions.

Having trouble getting new clients? Your ego will tell you it's the economy, the industry, the clients...externalizing the problem to blame it on anyone but you. But as a business owner, it is your duty and responsibility to kick your ego aside and pick apart your marketing materials, your selling techniques, your conversations and your mailing list to see what the problem is. Your ego helped you create these things and it's very proud of them in their current state. Don't let it talk you into staying the course when you aren't getting the desired results.

Ego Sugarcoats the Situation

It's the first question asked in every social setting – "How's business?" How are you answering that question? Are you being truthful or are you inflating your success to sound better? While I don't believe there is anything wrong with giving a sunny answer to Aunt Linda who doesn't know anything about your business and is just making conversation, you have to know when to get real and answer truthfully.

The first, and potentially most catastrophic, part of this problem is that your ego is likely preventing you from getting real with yourself. You may be sinking, but you just aren't ready to face it head on. As a business and marketing consultant, I have witnessed countless business owners deluding themselves for *years* about the status of their business. They just can't come clean and take responsibility to fix what's wrong.

The second part is that you are well aware of the gravity of the situation, but you aren't willing to be honest about it with the people who can help you. Being a strong leader means admitting you don't know it all and asking for help when you need it. When you allow your ego to steer, you choose to look only at the sugarcoated version of your business, causing you to miss valuable clues and opportunities. This doesn't work when you need advice and guidance from others. Get real about where you are and reach out to people who've been there before, so you can get the help you need to move forward.

Ego Prevents Authentic Connections

If your business isn't doing well, yet you pretend everything's OK when you speak to others, you miss opportunities to be authentically you—flaws and all—and make the valuable connections that get your business to a stronger place.

People are attracted to honesty and vulnerability. Admitting your problems and asking for help does not make you weak; it makes you human. When you let your ego lead, you wind up with "surface" business alliances – a straight exchange of needs, nothing more. To build a strong client base and a strong business, make as many *authentic connections* as possible. Make every client, every employee, every business partner and every vendor a die-hard fan. People are loyal to businesses with integrity. If they believe in what you're doing and how you're doing it, they will go above and beyond for you because they want to, not because it's in their contract. You can't develop that loyalty and trust when you are being led by your ego. (See Chapters 8 and 9 for more information on authentic connections.)

The Power of Your Beliefs

What are you thinking?

No, that's not a rhetorical question. If you want to build a profitable and sustainable practice, you need to pay attention to what you're thinking. Your thoughts become your beliefs and your beliefs can serve as the greatest catalyst to your success and fulfillment. On the flip side, they can also be the obstacles that prevent your success.

From the time you were little, you started forming beliefs and ideas about how life works. From everyday occurrences like darkness signaling bedtime to more personal situations, like how people reacted when you cried or got angry. Year after year, situation after situation, you built a belief system.

When you believe without a shadow of a doubt that something is true, your brain stops searching for alternate options and files that information in your subconscious under *"Complete."* You simply go about living your life knowing that this is the truth, operating in autopilot mode.

To expand your potential as a business owner, you will have to uncover and reconsider the "truths" that aren't serving you well anymore. Until you can convince yourself of an alternate truth, your belief will continue to hold you back.

Where you are right now in your business is a direct result of what you believe to be true. If you believe that you are having trouble getting new clients, you'll act accordingly. Believe you need two years to ramp up? That's how long it will take. But what if you believed that it would only take six months to ramp up? How would that change your actions?

Not until you begin to challenge your beliefs will you start to see that you have other options. And you always have other options—always.

Nowhere is this premise more significant than in the beliefs you have about your earning potential. Take a minute to consider what number would be an amazing salary for you to make next year. Write it down. What about the company's revenue next year? Write that down too.

What if you doubled those numbers? Or tripled them? Is that even conceivable? What are you telling yourself right now about that happening? These are all clues to how you may be limiting yourself.

All of us have a "cap" on what we believe we deserve to make and have. We have set the limit and we live by it. Fortunately, it's something that can shift as you gain confidence and new information, but many never question their self-imposed limits and therefore never move beyond them.

Consider how you reinforce these beliefs with what you say and if you need to expand or shift them, start by changing your dialogue. Here's a couple of specific ways to do that:

1. **Keep a journal**—Awareness is the first step to changing your dialogue.

Each time you catch yourself saying something that limits you—whether to yourself or out loud—write down what you said. Then write down what you *could have said* to not limit yourself. (e.g., "That client would never sign with me. My company's too small." Change it to "I would love to win a client like that. What advantage can I offer over the big firms?") Try out the new statement right away by saying it a few times and considering what actions you could take to back up this new way of thinking. If you keep this up, in time you will start automatically replacing the limiting statements with more productive ones.

2. **Get an accountability partner**—The ideal partner would be someone you interact with frequently.

Make a pact to call one another out every time one of you says something that is limiting or self-deprecating. You can create a secret signal to use if calling attention to the offense would be embarrassing, but make sure you challenge each other relentlessly. Eventually, you will start to catch yourself before the words even come out your mouth.

Dig deep into what you believe about your business and your ability to succeed as a business owner. Don't leave it to chance. Your beliefs are dictating your actions, so if you aren't seeing the results you want in your law firm, you owe it to yourself to investigate further.

The Value of Failure

I want you to fail. I'm serious. I really do.

Because the quicker you start failing, the quicker you can get to the place where you will succeed. Failures are funny like that.

One of the biggest tragedies of our modern culture is that we have a tendency to move forward as if everything is fine when it's not. Behind this phenomenon is a universal fear of talking about failure. *Why do we need failures?*

- Failures teach us lessons.

- Failures humble us.

- Failures breed connections.

No matter how many times people tell us something, and how incredibly passionate they are about their experience and what it taught them, often we don't learn until we feel the pain ourselves. It's much more profound when it happens to you. Building a legal practice will undoubtedly be the most valuable teaching experience in your career. You will have to step up and step out in ways you can't even imagine right now. And yes, you will fail sometimes. If failing scares you, you aren't alone, but know that it comes with the territory and that it will be your greatest teacher.

When I started in business, fellow business owners told me again and again to be very specific in my contracts, and to spell things out up front, to be sure expectations were clear. I was naïve and an eternal optimist, so I listened and agreed, but didn't fully heed the warning. It wasn't until I lost $14,000 on one job that this lesson really hit home. I neglected to clarify some terms up front and it burned me. This same job also gave me a lesson in trusting my gut. The client was trouble right from the start and I knew I should have turned the work away, but I saw dollar signs and proceeded against my better judgment. It was painful and embarrassing, but I never needed to be reminded about clarity in contracts – or trusting my gut – again. You too will go through similarly awful situations where you want to hide your head and cry (like I did), but you can always find a lesson or two to be learned once you come up for air.

I ran a successful marketing communications firm for nine years. Of course, there were failures, but it had many more successes. We won lots of awards, we had high profile clients, and I made a good salary from it. It also provided well for my staff. The second business I ran was not a success. After a couple of years, it just wasn't going in the direction my partner and I had envisioned, and quite frankly, neither of us was willing to commit the time, money or energy into getting it there. We cut our losses and closed it down. Was that the right decision? Absolutely, but it took me longer to come to terms with it than my partner because I was more attached to it . . . it was my baby. (Hello, Ego!) In retrospect, it was one of the best learning experiences of my career. It taught me that I know more than I was giving myself credit for; it taught me to look at selling in a different light; and it also taught me to open up about my failures. I had to talk about it. It was driving me crazy that I had failed. I talked to a therapist for the first time in my life. I talked to other women in my entrepreneurial network. Then a funny thing happened. I found out about *their* failures...the people who I thought had it made – big businesses, financial independence, and expert reputations. Every one of them had failed, and every one of them said that their failures were essential to the success they were experiencing now.

I admit I was worried that , when I went to these people with my tail between my legs, I would lose credibility . . . that they would never see me as an expert or trust that I could do anything right. After all, wasn't this proof that I sucked as a business owner? *I couldn't have been more off base.*

After I had openly admitted defeat and asked for help, I actually felt closer to them. We were connected by similar experiences. I even had several of them reach out to me to talk about working together. "Who, me? Didn't you hear me? I failed! I'm a failure." That's what I was saying in my head. But what they were hearing from me was, "I tried. It didn't work. Now I need your help to get me to the next step."

This is why you have to TALK about failures . . . because the voice in your head is seriously skewed against you. It's impossible to see things clearly and be objective when you're beating yourself up. I'm not saying you should talk about them for a year. But you need to spend enough time analyzing them to be able to answer these questions:

1. What lessons have I learned from this?

2. What connections have I made because of this? (Think people, as well as thoughts and ideas.)

3. Am I comfortable talking about this failure and if not, what is that saying about how I'm dealing with it?

4. How best can I proactively move beyond this and who can help me?

Once you embrace your failures, you become part of the club. (And yes, every successful business owner you can think of is in this club!) Strangely enough, looking back from the other side of it, you will find it both comforting and confidence boosting.

Don't fear failure. Celebrate the fact that you tried and learned, and that you are that much closer to succeeding.

Let me assure you right here and now, just because something you did hasn't worked out DOES NOT make you a failure. A failure is what happens; it's not who YOU are. Don't internalize it. See it for what is and move on.

Building a business is one of the most amazing experiences you can create for yourself. I can't imagine my life without it. It has taught me so much about myself, and I know that I have brought my own talents into the world in a bigger way having been at the steering wheel. I've stumbled. I've succeeded. I am thankful for every piece of strategic, tactical, and logistical piece of information I've acquired, but working through the *mental part* has been the toughest, yet most rewarding part. I suspect you will look back one day and say the same.

I wish you all the best as you build your legal practice. Here's to keeping your eyes open and your ego on a short leash.

About Tracy Dacko

Tracy Dacko has been involved in marketing and professional development for more than two decades. She has worked for both big companies and small, then in 2001, found her true calling and became a "serial entrepreneur." Throughout her entrepreneurial career, she has played an integral role in launching or expanding more than 50 companies, ranging from law firms and service-based consultancies, to medical schools, nonprofits and international corporations. Tracy is also part of the Esquire Coaching team.

Website: TheBusinessDistillery.com
Facebook: facebook.com/tracy.dacko
LinkedIn: linkedin.com/in/tracydacko

Chapter 13
Your Business Books: Clean or Crime Scene? Financial Tips for Non-Financial Emerging Solo and Small Firm Owners
by Donna Spina

I remember the moment I named my first company. "Thoroclean" popped into my head after a lengthy struggle for the perfect name. It happened while cleaning under a greasy sink in a busy restaurant kitchen. Having no background in business, I was naïve as to how much information and skill is required to sustain long-term success in self-employment. It was baptism by fire.

Starting a business with the intent to financially underwrite your life is something to be taken very seriously. Many people turn their passion into a business. But, being a great lawyer alone is not enough to create a successful business. Understanding your numbers reveals the sources of your income and expenses. They will crystallize your target audience (critical to creating business and marketing plans) and help you to set goals in order to continue the growth-in-earnings cycle. If this topic makes you cringe and your first impulse is to push this task onto another – STOP! As a business owner, knowing your numbers is YOUR responsibility; it will enable you to navigate your business with minimal surprises or setbacks.

In hindsight, there are two areas that would have had a significant positive impact on my own company's sustainability: accounting and knowing my target audience. Entire books are written on each of these topics. In this chapter, I will walk you through five steps to efficiently accomplish daily tasks and track your finances to improve profitability. After reading this chapter, continue to learn all that you can about these areas.

Step 1: Know Your Market

Realize and accept that, as a small firm owner, you are a sales person first. Without clients, you would not have the opportunity to practice law and generate money to support your firm and personal life. In order to effectively sell your services, you must really know your market (i.e., your ideal client base).

First, define your target audience. Frame the answer around these questions:

1. Will you be working directly with individuals, businesses, or vernmental entities? What are the particulars of each?

2. Where are they located (think of geography and where your target audience congregates, e.g., associations, senior centers, etc.)?

3. How large is this market in the states where you are barred?

4. If you work with individuals, what age group(s) is most suitable to your practice?

5. What income level is necessary to afford your fees?

6. What follow up is needed to address any challenges or difficulties your target market faces?

7. What are the trends in your market and in your area of law?

8. How are you going to stay in front of past clients so that they remember to refer or use your firm again in the future?

9. What did you learn unexpectedly during the research?

10. How can you put this information to work for you?

Note: The Chamber of Commerce, Bar Associations, local library references, professional or trade associations, and business database are great places to conduct research.

Step 2: Know How You Spend Your Time

Accounting is more than just numbers relating to how money is earned or spent. It also means being accountable to how you spend your time.

"Days are expensive. When you spend a day you have one less day to spend. So make sure you spend each one wisely."
−Jim Rohn

This wisdom applies to any new or existing businesses. Tasks are not just busy work. Their true purpose is to *strategically* move you forward toward your goal.

First, understand how your valuable time and strengths are spent by running the following questions through your mind regularly.

1. What really consumes most of your work time?

2. What dollar value can be assessed to it?

3. Is it busy work? If so, how necessary is this work?

4. Are you trying to avoid facing a less desirable task?

5. What could be done another time, in a more efficient fashion, or by someone else? (See Chapter 15 for more information on how to delegate to a dream team.)

Exercise Challenge #1— Task Time Management

To gain increased clarity to the answers to these questions, perform the following challenge.

1. Create a three column Log Sheet. Keep it by your side for easy access.

2. Label columns with Time, Task, and Level of Importance.

3. Divide the day into 15-minute intervals down the first column.

4. In the Task column, describe exactly what tasks you performed in each slot.

5. At the end of the day, critique the level of importance to see what was gainful forward moving to your business (GF), what was necessary busy work (NBW), and where you just spun your wheels (SW). Enter these evaluations in the third column.

6. Continue this assignment for one business week.

7. Design an Action Plan on how to deal with your fresh insight. If you're feeling too overwhelmed by your results, hire a Business Coach to assist in the Plan. Part of a Coach's role is to keep you on accountable to the Strategic Plan created.

Time	Task	Level of Importance
8:30 a.m.	Arrival to office	NBW
8:45 a.m.	Organize client notes from yesterday	NBW
9:00 a.m.	Review priority list for day	GF
9:15 a.m.	Reading e-mail	SW
9:30 a.m.	Reading e-mail	SW
9:45 a.m.	Reading e-mail	SW
10:00 a.m.	Get coffee and breakfast	SW

Without a boss or manager hovering over you with demands and steadfast deadlines, it is easy to get sidetracked when first self-employed. If yours is a home-based business, Exercise Challenge #1 will expose when you cross over during the business day into your personal life. Taking non-urgent calls from family and friends or doing the laundry should wait. Walking the dog should coincide with your scheduled breaks. Likewise, plan when you will attend a CLE or webinar to learn a new skill or strengthen an existing one.

To further help you efficiently manage time, try making lists. I am a list maker. Every end of business day, I compile or revise a list of prioritized tasks to complete the next day, by week's end, or month end. This way, my mornings start off more efficiently, with purpose, and with fewer last-minute surprises. (See Chapter 11 for more tips on time management.)

Step 3: Create Your Personal and Business Budgets

How much money do you truly need for the business to support itself first and you second? Good business practices start with how you manage your personal life. Working with the assumption that you have a single source of income, this shows you the exact amount of money you must bring home from the business (through a salary or owner's draw) to operate your personal life

Exercise Challenge #2-Determine Your Personal Budget

1. Create a spreadsheet. In the first column, list all your personal expenses: rent or mortgage, real estate taxes, car loan or lease, utilities (heating or cooling energy, telephone, cable, water/sewer, food, gasoline, insurances (auto, home, health, life), credit card, and anything else paid during a month or over the year.

2. In the heading, enter each month of the year horizontally across the top.

3. Now fill in every space corresponding to a certain expense and the month incurred until you have filled in the entire spreadsheet. Use the billing due date as a guideline. Late charges, interest, or penalties erode your operating capital. Some expenses will be recurring (like rent or mortgage payments) and others will be due at particular times of the year (like installment payments for insurance coverage). If you don't know a specific amount, estimate.

4. Customize the worksheet so that the columns add the data entered down and the individual rows are added across. This will provide totals per expense item and per month.

5. This is the "Personal Budget" you have intentionally or unintentionally drafted for yourself. Review the Budget you have created. Any changes needed? What are you missing?

6. Time to compare. If you have not yet started taking a salary, this budget informs you the minimum amount of money you need to bring home each month. If you are already taking a salary from your business, look at the Year-to-Date totals on your most recent pay stub. What is the Gross amount paid to you? What is the Net?

a. How does this Net compare to your Personal Budget total over the same time period? Ideally, using a 12-month calendar year creates a clearer picture.

b. Is it higher or lower?

c. If higher, you have spent more than you truly earn. Your credit card debt is probably hiding the difference. If less, you have a positive cash flow, meaning a surplus exists to create reserves for an emergency or savings, or to reinvest in your business.

2014	January	February	March	April	May	ITEM TOTALS
Accountant				250.00		250.00
Auto Insurance		225.00			225.00	450.00
Cable TV	150.00	150.00	150.00	150.00	150.00	750.00
Cell Phone	125.00	125.00	125.00	125.00	125.00	625.00
Credit Card	998.79	678.12	645.13	704.56	816.74	3843.34
Rent	1525.00	1525.00	1525.00	1525.00	1525.00	7625.00
COLUMN TOTALS:	2798.79	2703.12	2445.13	2754.56	2841.74	13543.34

Once you've determined your personal budget, it's time to determine your annual business budget. An annual Budget is a reasonable forecast of anticipated itemized income and expenses in the month or year in which they will occur. Your first budget is the most challenging being more a logical guess until your business creates a history. An annual budget is most effective when it has: (1) an Actual column, reflecting the true expense; (2) a Projected Budget column, which is what you predicted to earn or spend in that same category and time period; and (3) a Variance Column, which shows the difference between your actual and projected budgets.

Budgeting is a financial plan. It shows preliminary expenses, proposed income, operating expenses (monthly or periodically over the year), cash flow (positive or negative), and reserves to overcome shortfalls or roll over from year to year.

Exercise Challenge #3—Determine Your Business Budget

Create a new spreadsheet. Follow the instructions from Exercise #2. This time, however, list only the Expenses that pertain to your business. Be sure to include expenses such as business and payroll taxes, staff salaries, and fees to independent contractors (e.g., accountant).

In a separate document, you will want to keep track of your assets and liabilities. An asset is something of monetary value that the business owns or has acquired. It can be physical in nature, such as cash, real estate, inventory, and equipment. It can also be something intangible such as right (copyright or trademark). If you are a startup, many assets will be purchased. Pricing and specifications are needed for the purchases of furniture (desks, chairs, storage cabinetry, conference table and chairs), phones, computer, printer, copier, some decorations, and other forms of technology or software.

A liability is the financial obligation a business has to its owners, short or long term loans, wages payable, leases, taxes, and more arising out of past or current transactions. "Liabilities" could include: office or equipment leases, business loan payments, maintenance of equipment, printed marketing materials (business cards, brochures, letter head, envelopes, branding), business and payroll incomes taxes, additional insurances, and other office supplies.

Whether you are a new lawyer or a seasoned professional, all business owners must keep meticulous records for each expenditure. That includes any use of personal funds for business reasons, mileage logs, receipts for meals with prospects or clients, and more. In the event of an audit, never trust your memory. Be sure to include a brief description of names, places, and purpose for each receipt. Without conscientious attention, you risk understating your actual business costs and missing deductions on your tax return.

Caution: *Never* commingle business funds with your personal account. Regardless of the legal entity, it is imperative that these two accounts remain separate. Any withdrawal from the business account must be clearly defined in the memo section or in computerized accounting by coding to justify the trail from business to personal or the vice versa. Ideally, set up a separate credit card used exclusively for business purposes.

Step 4: Cash Flow Considerations

Now that you have a good idea as to the expense requirements for both sides of your life, the next step is to be mindful of cash flow considerations. Essentially, managing cash flow is about ensuring that you have enough money coming in to cover the expenses that are going out.

First, determine your gross revenue: the money needed to not only cover, but to also exceed all of your personal and business expenses. To determine the **minimum** *gross annual revenue*:

Annual Personal Expenses + Annual Business Expenses + 10% Buffer (for cost overruns or client turnover/loss)

To help you determine your average monthly revenue goals, divide the minimum gross annual revenue by 12.

The goal of every business is to generate a Profit. Profit is the surplus that remains once all business expenses are paid. Your first objective is to hit your minimum gross annual revenue goal. Once that is met, you can focus on increasing profits.

In order to have positive cash flow, you will need to meet or exceed your gross revenue goals on a monthly basis. In order to help you meet your gross revenue goals, let's first evaluate how you're generating income. Answer the following:

1. What is your fee structure (e.g., billable hour, retainer, etc.) and what are your fees?

2. What factors determined your fee structure?

3. Who are your competitors?

4. How do you compare to your competitors in price, quality of service, reliability, or expertise?

5. What do you offer that is unique to you? How can you leverage this in your fees/fee structure?

Most lawyers charge clients an hourly rate (billable hour). While a billable hour is standard industry practice, consider grouping your services together in a good, better, best packaging with an increasing price tag attached, or finding a way to offer a flat fee or retainer program. It is easier to maintain positive cash flow and estimate monthly revenue when offering these types of fee structures in addition to your hourly rate. Once you've evaluated your fee structure and adjusted it based on the information gathered, determine how many clients are needed from every fee category to attain each month's revenue goal.

We are assuming that the clients are paying at the time services are rendered. Not all will. Answer the following questions to help you better manage your monthly cash flow:

1. What other methods of payment would you offer in order to keep your pipeline of ideal clients full?

2. How many more regularly paying clients would you need to provide a cushion when waiting for payments from others?

3. Would a business line of credit be a safer hedge to even out cash flow?

4. Will you accept cash, check, or credit card?

5. Will you extend credit to your clients periodically or routinely?

6. What screening requirements must they meet to qualify?

7. What will be your collections policies and procedures?

8. How will you monitor payments or finance charges for late payments?

9. How will you track your accounts receivable (incoming money)?

Unfortunately, not every penny you bring in is yours. A significant piece is reserved for income taxes, both business and personal. There are a variety of deadlines for specific tax filings such as payroll and personal estimated. Missing these deadlines, not following the specific governmental rules, will result in steep penalties with hefty interest charges. It is best to consult your accountant regularly, perhaps every three months or sooner depending on the size and speed of your business' growth. Large, unexpected expenses are never a good surprise. Meeting these high financial demands in a short time frame will adversely impact your cash flow, creating a domino effect with other routine obligations.

Step 5: Have a System to Stay on Track

You do not need to be a Certified Public Accountant (CPA), but you do need to learn financial basics and organization. That starts with a simple system, usually accounting software, which is the one place where all the data, general business and client information, is recorded. There are many accounting programs available. If not already tailored to your type of business, it can be customized with your practice area's language. Unless you are already familiar with these types of programs, the learning curve and time investment can be reduced by enrolling in classes and trainings, rather than attempting to be self-taught.

Accounting software also can generate reports in which you can pick the time frame (daily, weekly, monthly, yearly) for viewing purposes. There are three basic but key reports that properly utilized software will generate: Balance Sheet, Profit and Loss (P & L) Statement, and Cash Flow Statement.

1. Balance Sheet—is a snapshot for a specific time period. It states the Assets owned by the entity, how it paid for them, liabilities owed, and what equity remains. Any lender will request this report for an entity's true financial condition. Its fundamental accounting equation is:

$$Assets = Liabilities + Owners\ Equity$$

When these numbers are not equal, an error exists or the business might be in harm's way. Seek out professional guidance.

2. Profit and Loss Statement—is based on the fundamental accounting equation:

$$Income = Revenue - Expenses$$

Each part of the formula is itemized corresponding to a certain month, quarter, or year. The ending number is Net Income (Profit or Loss). This report guides the business owner on how to improve results to increase profitability.

3. Cash Flow Statement reports—where the entity's money went, incoming and outgoing, during a pre-determined period of time. It breaks down operating, investing, and financing activities, showing how changes in the Balance Sheet affect cash. Profit is not the same as cash.

$$Out\ of\ cash = Out\ of\ Business$$

It is important to become familiar with the financial terminology your accountant and software will use. The terms "Assets" and "Liabilities" have already been defined in this chapter. Some additional terms include:

Equity reflects the ownership claim or interest for a business.

Accounts Receivable (A/R) is earned income from services rendered or sale of goods but unpaid by your clients. Every company's mission is to collect these timely and in full.

Accounts Payable (A/P) are unpaid bills (liabilities) owed to suppliers that are short term. Lenders and Investors examine this category to judge the soundness of the entity's daily financial management.

Understanding and appreciating the numbers, and developing a healthy respect for the money in your business, can mean the difference between being a bankruptcy attorney and being the client of one.

About Donna Spina

Donna J. Spina, ACC, CPC, ELI-MP, is a Professional, Workplace, Personal Growth, & Career Transition Coach. Her unique and creative coaching process includes the use of well-respected Behavioral and Energy Assessments that help her clients learn more about themselves, self-discover their purpose and passion, and better relate and communicate with others while integrating work into their lives. Donna is also on the Esquire Coaching team.

Website: CoachingInDeed.com
Facebook: facebook.com/CoachingInDeed
LinkedIn: linkedin.com/pub/donna-j-spina-acc-cpc-eli-mp/9/540/62b

Chapter 14
8 Steps to Hiring Your Dream Team
by Melody Stevens

In order to grow your law practice, you're likely going to need a support team to assist you with things like administration, reception, research, maybe with cases in a different specialty than yours and the like. I say "the like" because I don't know squat about the ins and outs of law. However, I do know a lot about businesses that require an administrative support team. This chapter is written for anyone who is considering hiring one or more people for his or her practice, whether it's an associate, paralegal, administrative professional or another partner. (As a lawyer, you probably know more than I do about the various types of business partnerships one can have. My experience is with employees. I've never had a formal business partner, but I have successfully hired many people with more professional experience and education than I have.)

I own a music and dance school in New Jersey and a preschool in New York. Both businesses have an administrative front office as well as professional teachers on both junior and senior levels. I generally don't work on site at either location. One major reason is, that after a lot of hard knocks, I've figured out some secrets to having dream teams of employees that I can trust to handle all the customer service, sales, administration and even all the teaching. (I'm a music teacher by trade and I've been able to hire people who are as good as or better than me at teaching in my music and dance school. I've also hired some fabulous early childhood teachers at my preschool.)

My current job, in short, is to keep my enterprise growing, to make big executive decisions, to open as many locations as I want, to close locations that aren't profitable or aren't working, to keep on top of industry trends, to train the leaders of my company (managers, lead teachers, and directors) to be the best they can be, to keep learning, to continually strategize, and to keep evolving as a person. Big job, but it makes me so happy!

Please note that my job did not start out this way. I was the sole voice, piano, and Kindermusik teacher in my business, doing my own bookkeeping, scheduling, most of the customer service and most other tasks in my business 80 hours a week for years. I learned over time that I was at my best for everyone when I stepped out of the things I didn't enjoy doing and hire out. My company grew exponentially as a result of my sticking to things I either loved doing or that required high mental energy and my particular talents without tons of distractions.

I'm telling you all this partly because I want you to dream as big as you want. What if you only handled your very favorite types of cases, for example, and you had people working with or for you that handled the rest? What if you had a team of people in your front office who screened your calls, kept your office impeccably clean and organized, and informed you of your schedule day after day, joyfully?

So how do you pull together your dream team? I'll take you step by step!

Step 1: Assess Your Immediate Needs

Get something to write or type on and:

1. List your absolute favorite things you currently do for your practice. Then, look at the list and highlight the things that require a high level of thinking, talent and/or education.

2. List everything else you do for your practice, and I mean *everything*. Spill it. Even cleaning the toilet. (Unless that's already in list #1, but that would just be weird to me.)

3. List things that should be done but aren't getting done.

Take the items that aren't highlighted in list #1, plus the whole of lists #2 and #3, and make two columns. Column #1 is called "Administrative tasks." This would be for perhaps a personal assistant, receptionist, or a cleaning person. Column #2 is called "Professional tasks." These would be for someone with more specific legal training; perhaps a paralegal, an associate, or even a partner to come on board with you. Write all the tasks in their respective columns. These are your immediate needs.

Now, what is your best guess as to how many hours a week each of these columns requires? If it's more than two hours a week per column, you have a job for someone other than you. Less than two hours, you can keep the tasks to yourself, *for now*.

TIPS:

• Underestimate the number of hours you'll need from a prospective employee. Most people prefer to be offered more hours later because you've underestimated than to be cut back because you've overestimated the job. And, there's nothing worse than paying someone to twiddle their thumbs. Trust me.

• Keep administrative and professional/legal as separate people. No one is great at everything. Consider, too, depending on the amount of administrative tasks you need done, two part-time people like an office manager and a bookkeeper and/or a cleaning person rather than one "everything" person.

Step 2: Write Your Job Description(s)

There are many schools of thought about job descriptions. Some say less is more, some say more is more. I say it depends. I've had the best luck with the "more is more" philosophy (list tasks) when going for managerial, administrative, or sales-type employees, and I've had the best luck with the "less is more" philosophy with professional/technical/teacher type employees, which for you would be fellow lawyers (listing tasks would be insulting to these candidates).

Sample Administrative Job Description:

Busy lawyer seeks an administrative assistant for the following tasks:

(List column #1 tasks)

The job is approximately 25 hours a week and is to be on-site. E-mail cover letter and resume.

Sample Professional Job Description:

Busy lawyer seeks an associate with the following experience and credentials:

_____.

Must have an interest in _____ law.
E-mail cover letter and resume.

Step 3: Decide How Much You'll Pay

Contrary to popular belief, hiring someone at a higher wage and better benefits will *not* guarantee you a dream team employee. In fact, many people who want to leave or have left their jobs looking for higher pay are way too mercenary ("in it for the paycheck") to employ in a happy law practice. And they will leave you at the smell of more money elsewhere. (I'm not saying that people shouldn't look to improve their financial circumstances. I'm saying that in your small business, if you're in the beginning stages of hiring, you may not have the resources to pay top dollar, and you don't have to.)

I've found that it's often better to hire someone at lower, but fair-for-your-industry wages and along the way you can perhaps create a bonus system, both planned and unplanned, to thrill them. Bonuses are performance-based and also based on the financial health of your practice. This is an example of "under-promising and over-delivering" which is a great business practice any time.

Often, the best, most loyal employees are willing to start out at "entry level" wages. Consider, also, if it fits the tasks you need done, a minimum wage, eager intern professionally or administratively who has the potential to grow with your company.

Step 4: Advertise the Position

There are several ways to do this (which I've had success with in the past).

1. Post the job description(s) online. I like Indeed.com. My second favorite is craigslist.org.

2. Talk to your family and friends regarding what you are seeking.

3. Call two or three staffing agencies. You may pay more up front, but it's a good option to try.

4. If you're considering an intern, offer a paid (minimum wage) internship on internships.com.

Here is a tip about interns: although many of my colleagues argue with me, I prefer to hire paid versus unpaid interns. You avoid a lot of red tape and potential labor department hassles doing it this way as opposed to getting a free intern.

Step 5: Screen Cover Letters and Resumes and Do a First Interview with All Viable Prospects

Do not offer a position to anyone just from a cover letter or resume or from the first interview without completing all of the steps in this chapter.

A cover letter that's more about you than about them is a good sign.

Wondering how to interview? Well, it is safe to say that it's not so much about the exact questions you ask, as it is about trusting your gut about a person after you've spent time in conversation with them. You're the lawyer, so make sure you don't ask any illegal questions, but really, don't get too caught up with what you ask. It's more about how you feel around them that counts.

Here's where it gets fun for me! How can you tell a dream team employee from the polar opposite, who I'd call a "serenity buster?"

Following is a blog post that I wrote for SavortheSuccess.com on characteristics to look for when searching for a dream team employee.

Blog Post:

In the past, I used to look for certain traits when making my decision to hire an employee. These included:

-Great credentials

-Entrepreneurial spirit

-Excellent technical skills

-Great enthusiasm for the job at hand

-Someone who could bring in their own clients

And, I can tell you unequivocally, I failed miserably in building a dream team based on the above characteristics. More often than not, I got serenity busters. And, so here is my "David Letterman" top 10 list for traits of a dream-team employee. Here goes!

10. Cares about the way they dress

9. Gets along well with coworkers

8. Allows you, the owner, to be you—no unsolicited harsh criticisms- although they can and should point out if you've made a mistake that could harm the company, or if you're in a negative pattern that is bringing down company morale.

7. Has your back. (For instance, they'll make sure you don't forget stuff, and when you do, they will handle it for you.)

6. Has hobbies, other interests, family, friends and a life outside of your business

5. Is great with people

4. Speaks eloquently (necessary in customer service positions, not in all jobs)

3) Is in their "fun" or "self-expression" in whatever position they are in for your company

2) Is a cheerful person in general

And . . . drum roll please! The #1 characteristic of a dream team employee is . . .

The ability to grow and change with the company and with the job

A successful company is a constantly morphing and changing, creative entity. People who cannot deal with change will never be a dream team employee. Those who dig their heels in or freak out at a change of paint color or even a change of personnel can bust your serenity and hold your company back. Have you ever known a company that has truly stood the test of time that hasn't changed? Of course not.

You want to have a conversation with the prospective employee about relationships like former coworkers, business associates and friends. Also talk about their outside interests and hobbies.

As for the "serenity busters," well, I've identified some classic personality types and several tips on how to spot them on a resume or in an interview. These are my top three most common serenity-busting employees (there are several more, less common). Don't hire these people, please.

The Owner-Wannabe

They will tell you they want to have their own practice just like yours one day. They will use the phrase "In my experience . . . " or something like that, often. You'll feel compelled to hire them and mentor them and you'll fall in love with their entrepreneurial spirit and camaraderie. However, if you hire this type of employee, chances are you will start mentoring them as they work for you and you'll seek much advice from them. Then, inevitably, something will happen and you will have to put your foot down or make some sort of significant change in your company without getting their "buy in." They will then start getting resentful and jealous of you and your authority and start to sabotage you and your practice consciously or unconsciously. Ugh.

Note: A great intern is different because he or she is content to start at entry level and work their way up the ranks. It's more the professional lawyer or office manager type that you need to watch out for if they say any of the above things.

The Ever-Innocent Flake

They are very often late or absent from work and they have such excuses that you'd feel guilty calling them out on the un-reliability. Excuses include but are not limited to: "My kid just fell down the stairs." "I just got into a car accident." "My mother is in the hospital." "My babysitter no-showed on me and I have no one to watch my kids today." "I just threw up." "I have the stomach flu."

The excuses are endless and they sound so real at the time. Maybe sometimes they are real, but this type of person often attracts negativity and doesn't belong in your happy law practice.

Of course if they miss the interview due to one of these excuses, do NOT go out of your way to reschedule. Let them come to you.

Also, check their resume thoroughly to see how long they were at the jobs. An ever-innocent flake often stays in jobs for a short period of time...I wonder why?

In the interview, watch out for extreme over-the-top enthusiasm for the job. This means they are thinking with the right (emotional) side of the brain only and the left (logical) side hasn't kicked in. Extreme enthusiasm isn't good. There should be some fear or skepticism about something, or at least some logical questions asked by the prospective employee.

The Prima Donna

Their classic line is "Have you seen my resume?" This person is so full of ego they are unemployable. They either won't hold on to clients and blame your business practices for it, or worse, they will hold onto clients like glue and bust your serenity behind the scenes so when you ultimately fire them, you risk losing the clients who, not knowing any better, will follow them.

If they lose clients, they will say to you: "Have they seen my resume?"

Watch out for someone who talks and talks about themselves without asking you questions about the job. Also watch out for feeling compelled to please them and to justify yourself in the interview. This is a very bad sign. Never, ever, ever hire someone you feel you need to "talk into the job."

Step 6: Get and Check References

This is so important and it's a step so many employers skip. Please, please don't be lazy because this step is probably the most telling as to who you're hiring. I like to get three personal and three professional references. I've avoided hiring many potential serenity busters because they didn't or couldn't provide me with these. On the contrary, some if not all of my best employees had many stellar references. Recently, I hired one of the references of one of my dream team employees! She (the reference) is now also one of my dream-teamers!

Make sure you actually call and speak with at least two personal and two professional references.

Here's a tip: if you bond with someone's references over the phone that's a very good sign!

Step 7: Have a Final Interview with Another Person Present

Have a second and final interview with at least one other person present (your friend, colleague, mentor, spouse . . . anyone you trust).

Okay, this is where the candidate needs to tell you why they would love to take the job. Remember, no convincing. They need to convince you. Why are they the best candidate for the job over the many you've interviewed? (I credit my preschool mentor Bobbie Robertson with this tip.)

Both you and the person you trust with you must like the candidate for the job. If one of you is a thumbs down, it's a no-go.

Step 8: Make an Offer!

It's time to offer the job to the candidate. There should be no negative surprises because in the job description and in the interviews, you've been under-promising and you've done nothing to convince the person to take the job.

If anything, if the prospective employee has passed all the above tests and you feel in your gut this person is super right for you, this may be the time to "up the ante" if that could thrill the candidate and make it easy for them to take the job. I've done things like throw in reimbursed bus fare, parking fees, or, if I know the candidate will need to get childcare, I have thrown in some extra money in the wage or salary so they can afford that.

If they accept the job, write up a contract with no promise of length of employment, but with the terms and conditions of the job and the offer on it. Both you and the employee sign and date the contract, but I don't need to be telling you this because you're the lawyer!

And with your dream team in place, I wish you a very happy law practice!

About Melody Stevens

Melody Stevens says that the best teachers in business (and life) are the ones who have made the most colossal mistakes, and have lived to tell about them. A 14-year veteran music studio owner (now with two locations), NYC preschool owner, singer, consultant, mother, wife, and homeowner, Melody has received an incredible business and life education and is here to share. Melody is also a contributing author for the Huffington Post, and author of Become a Time Millionaire.

Website: MelodyStevens.net
Facebook: facebook.com/TimeMillionaire
Twitter: @timemillion

Chapter 15
Celebrate Your Team
by Jill Magerman

"There were four people, named Everybody, Somebody, Anybody and Nobody. There was an important job to be done. Everybody was asked to do it. Everybody was sure Somebody would do it. Anybody could have done it, but Nobody did it. Somebody got angry about that, because it was Everybody's job. Everybody thought Anybody could do it, but Nobody realized that Everybody wouldn't do it. It ended up that Everybody blamed Somebody when Nobody did what Anybody could have done."
— Principles of Team Work, Author Unknown

After asking countless lawyers whom I know about the teamwork in their law firms and getting a look of confusion and unfamiliarity, I realized that I had hit on something. Law firms don't necessarily support teamwork. Most practices operate in the "every man (or woman) for himself" principle. Yes, some said, "We have a great team. We go out, go on retreats, have incentives that promote healthy competition and we get along." While those are group experiences, it is not a model for practicing law. Each of those lawyers is still working on his or her cases in a vacuum, rarely bringing on other lawyers from the firm.

What is teamwork as it relates to a law practice? By definition, teamwork in a law firm environment means partnering with other lawyers and support staff in the firm to reach common goals. With teamwork, it is the firm that is promoted, and it is the firm that is the legal representative of clients, not any single lawyer. In Sally

Kane's work, entitled *Top Ten Legal Skills*, she notes that teamwork skills include:

- Collaborating with others to reach a common goal

- Coordinating and sharing information and knowledge

- Cultivating relationships with colleagues, staff, clients, experts, vendors and others

- Attending and participating in team events, meetings and conferences

There are many examples of successful law practices that work as a team and this can be achieved both in large and small firms. In the larger firms it is likely to occur when the practice is divided into departments. Each department handles cases in a particular area of law. These departments have their "rainmaker," usually a senior partner, and that player oversees all the delegation and work that happens on an individual case. In smaller firms, where there are a few partners and a small group of support staff, cases can be handled by the entire team of lawyers. In those models, you play to the strength of each lawyer. For example, if one partner is particularly skillful at client relations and another is great at organization and triaging, the role of each partner is clear, but they each play for the same team and on the same cases.

In many firms teams just don't exist. Many lawyers are competitive by nature and want to be the very best in the firm. This is encouraged, since it directly impacts the revenue for the firm. Because of the economy, both cost containment and unprecedented personnel cutbacks have increased the emphasis on producing a high number of revenue-generating clients. Those lawyers that survive are living in a culture of fear and scarcity. Protecting one's own security has become paramount. Historically, many law firms have discovered that you can truly make a lot of money if you work everybody very, very hard and really slash your costs and don't care about how people—partners, associates, or staff—feel about their work lives.

Large firms are often still enjoying success, but for some, the big firm environment has become increasingly unsatisfying. There is so much emphasis on maximizing billable hours that it not only strips lawyers of their enjoyment of work, but it certainly discourages teamwork and true collaboration.

What's the incentive to change? Why mess with success?

"Talent wins games, but teamwork and intelligence wins championships." —Michael Jordan

First and foremost, according to Ed Poll, attorney and coach, "team efforts produce greater revenues, both for the firm and for the individuals." This is contrary to the popular conception. Clients unfamiliar with your firm look for the overall success with the entire practice, not necessarily the individual wins. Branding the achievements of the firm as a whole is easier than segregating multiple individual accomplishments.

A second benefit to teamwork is that multiple minds are frequently better than one. The creative process that happens when collaboration occurs is greater than that of working through the process alone.

A third benefit is that there is an overall increase in compassion and understanding among the partners, associates and support staff. When you consistently work intimately with your colleagues it's hard to ignore that each person is deeper than what he or she brings to work. That compassion and understanding translates directly to your clients. They see your human side too.

While there are many compelling reasons to explore, one final benefit that is often overlooked is employee satisfaction. Happy employees work longer, harder and more effectively. The work environment is important and can have significant impact on how the lawyers show up each day. Happy lawyers connect and relate to their clients better. This relationship is what will endure and will foster client satisfaction and repeat and referral business.

One lawyer interviewed reported that she really enjoys coming to work every day. She is a member of a true team approach in the practice where she is one of three partners. They each know their strengths and can lean on the other partners in areas that they are weak. A client knows that he or she is hiring the firm, not an individual lawyer when he or she hires them. They are all about the entire practice and not individual accomplishment. Likewise, in a solo practice, a client's needs are better served when a team of support staff can help the lawyer play to his or her strengths, while the staff takes care of the administrative details.

Because of all the persuasive reasons to move to a team approach, there is a movement to make a paradigm shift. But if a firm wants to promote "teamwork," that usually means that the law firm culture must change. Making a change is a process. An atmosphere of collaboration doesn't materialize overnight.

Firms can work toward this culture by making teamwork a core value and striving to create an open, inclusive environment that fosters learning and values each team member. The following tips can help your firm pave the way to a more connected and collaborative culture.

Lead by Example

There's hardly anything worse for a firm's morale than leaders who practice the "do as I say, not as I do" policy. The managing partner or practice group leader needs to reach out to other lawyers for their expertise. Can you imagine the impact on both the bottom line and the quality of work produced when assignments are appropriately delegated?

Mentor

Mentoring goes hand in hand with leading by example. What a great way to have junior lawyers integrate with your team. This is an opportunity to pair a novice lawyer with a more seasoned lawyer—to share his or her experience—not only in lawyering skills but to acclimate the newcomer to the culture of your firm. Similarly, a solo practitioner can reach out to other lawyers through the bar association to both receive and provide mentoring, which in turn, can increase cross-referrals.

Focus on Client Needs/Satisfaction

In an interview with *Law Practice*, Kenneth Carroll, a founding partner of Morningstar Law Group, said, "At Morningstar, we have tried to eliminate that internal tension and competition, which ultimately has nothing to do with client service. All clients are viewed as firm clients, not the individual lawyer's client. We believe that philosophy encourages the correct approach, whereby the most appropriate lawyer in the firm handles each particular matter for the client." By collaborating to ensure the best possible client outcome, firms enhance their reputation and profitability.

Transparency and Openness

Quint Studer, author of the book *Straight A Leadership: Alignment, Action, Accountability* asserts that companies with cultures of openness and free-flowing information fare better in difficult economies. That's because (among other benefits) transparency helps employees stay connected to the financial big picture, reduces complacency, sparks creative solutions, creates organizational consistency and stability, and leads to faster, more efficient execution.

A more collaborative spirit will arise when leadership shares what is going on with clients, cases and the business aspects including the long range plans for the practice. There are obvious limits to what can be shared, but an open environment leads to decreased fears. Most people are afraid of what they don't know, but can handle challenges when confronted directly with them. If everyone knows what's going on, collaboration on what's there is a natural process if it is encouraged.

Revisit or Create Your Mission Statement and Values of Your Firm

Does your firm or practice have a working mission statement? Is it just a framed document that is plastered to a wall collecting dust? Take time to revisit your mission statement (or help create one if none exists). How close is your practice today to the one that existed when this document was written?

A mission statement should not have flowery words that are recited only on special occasions, but it should be a document that is a working manuscript that reflects the values and standards of your firm. You want each lawyer to read this and feel an immediate connection to why they are at this firm.

When you sit down to revisit your mission statement take time to see if teamwork is one of your stated values. In Sally Kane's work entitled, *Top Ten Legal Skills*, she includes Teamwork as one of the ten.

Develop a DPA, Designed Partnership Agreement

This internal document is intended to have all the players be clear about the expectations pertaining to the culture of that particular law practice. It is like the rules of the game. This agreement spells out how the team members want the relationships in the practice to be. It is also designed to describe what happens when things don't go as expected. In this agreement, the attention is on what the members can commit to, not to how they want others to be. It is best to use an outside facilitator or coach to co-create this document.

Connecting to Your Heart and Your Passion

Band of Bearded Brothers™ is a documentary that was created about the 2013 Major League Baseball World Series contenders. As a way to strengthen their bond with each other, they each grew their beards and they formed this team's unique identity and helped restore the faith of the Red Sox Nation™. A World Series championship resulted. As their beards grew so did their connection to what they were passionate about. They put so much heart and soul into their playing. It was truly a team effort.

Growing beards in your firm isn't necessarily how your practice will form its team and some of the women lawyers might be additionally challenged to join this bonding. However, connecting to what does speak to each one's heart and then matching it with the mission of the firm will ultimately move the practice to a more collaborative culture.

Reward Collaboration

In order to do this, there must also be consideration to shift the compensation structure. Currently most practices reward only individual achievement of billable hours. In this shift, the law practice, supported by the firm's leadership, must explicitly state that a requirement of being a member of the firm is that other members of the firm be involved in their cases as appropriate. The specifics of that involvement and process of compensation needs to be developed by each firm, but base compensation must, in some fashion, be tied to the effectiveness of the lawyer involving other firm lawyers or practice groups as part of the team delivering legal services to clients.

Recognition and Appreciation

As teams proliferate, organizations must shift the emphasis of their recognition programs from individual to team rewards. Even individual rewards should acknowledge people who are effective team players -- people who freely share their expertise, "share their clients," help out when needed, and challenge teams to improve. Firms need to get away from a star system that rewards only the individuals who stand out from the group, and also reward people who help the crowd perform better. In addition, there needs to be an environment that regularly demonstrates appreciation for the contributions that all team members make.

Team PLAY

While most of the focus of this chapter has been on team*work*, team *play* is an important aspect to consider in all law practices. It might seem obvious that creating a pleasant work environment is what all practices strive for, but that doesn't happen without intentional thought and planning. Bringing in lunch, celebrating a colleague's birthday, holiday parties, going out after work for drinks, having contests and even working together on charity events are all ways to boost morale and to develop a sense of a team at work. Team building activities sometimes get a bad rap. The ropes course, scavenger hunts and relay races seem to some a waste of time, but time spent away from the day-to-day work schedule can forge and strengthen valuable relationships. Even the occasional good-spirited prank can change the atmosphere in an office especially when schedules and deadlines have been tight. One practice shared that once when a partner was out for a couple days, the other partners and associates filled the absent partner's office with the firm's logo-imprinted balloons. There was no room to move in the office. Maybe the partner was known for being full of hot air?

Teams need to be supported. It is not only important to build and maintain teams within your practice, but knowing who your support system is beyond the workplace is key to succeeding both professionally and personally, especially for sole proprietors. Who can you count on? Who has your back? Who will challenge you in service of making you a better person? Who gives you that "atta boy"? These are all members of your "Fan Club" (term borrowed from Dillon Marcus, *Executive Retreats*). They cheer you on and push you to be your best. These are team members that go beyond your work associates. The support you get outside of work impacts directly on the success and satisfaction you experience at work. Who is in the front row of your bleachers?

Teamwork and team play culture happens only if the leadership values them. Once the benefits of working as a team are accepted, the shift can happen by following the tips described in this chapter. Like any team, leadership is key. If the quarterback leads his or her teammates by trusting the talent he or she has and including the team in decision making and planning, the individuals will play and work their hardest for the outcome of the entire team, not just their own personal accomplishments. While this isn't a completely linear process, overall, teamwork and team play increase lawyer satisfaction, which leads to increased client satisfaction, which leads to increased revenue.

"Coming together is a beginning. Keeping together is progress. Working together is success." —*Henry Ford*

About Jill Magerman

With her energetic and wildly creative personality, Jill brings a special combination of skills and talents to her work as the co-founder and Certified Professional Coach for atrio Professional Life Coaches. Whether it is a career, relationship or life stage change, Jill provides the tools needed for living a greater, more passionate life. When working with individuals, groups or while designing and facilitating workshops, she conveys her message with love, humor and humility.

Website: atriolifecoaches.com
Website: Meaningful-Milestones.com
Facebook: facebook.com/atriocoaches
LinkedIn: linkedin.com/pub/jill-magerman/11/485/851
Twitter: @atriocoachjill

P art IV

Cultivating Peace of Mind

Chapter 16
Stress: The Best and Worst Thing in Your Life
by Jason Rodriguez

Stress—"a state of mental or emotional strain or tension, resulting from adverse or demanding circumstances" (Oxford).

This is an extremely limited definition to one of the most complex words in the dictionary. Stress involves our reaction to an outside stimulus. Since we all react differently to different situations there is no direct definition of what stress is because it's all based on perception.

In this chapter I'm going to show you some different forms of stress, ways stress can have adverse effects on your health, and some symptoms of being overly stressed. More importantly, I'm going to give you concrete tips on how to decrease the bad stress in your life, improve your overall health, and embrace the good stress in your life to create a healthier, more productive, happier you.

Hundreds of millions of years ago, a caveman was leaving his cave to find food for his family. He realized he might never return because predators ran rampant upon the earth. As he prepared to exit the cave, his heart pounded, his muscles grew tense, his blood pressure rose, his breath quickened, and his senses grew sharper. These physical changes increased his stamina, reaction time, strength, speed, and enhanced his focus preparing him to fight or flee from danger.

On June 14, 1998 Michael Jordan was playing in game six of the NBA finals. The Chicago Bulls were losing 86-83 to the Utah Jazz with only 41.9 seconds left. There was no question who the ball was going to. Jordan scored a lay-up and then stole the ball from Karl Malone, drove up the court, and scored a jump shot with 5.1 seconds left to win the game and his 6th NBA championship. Michael Jordan is considered the greatest basketball player of all time because he performed better than anyone else in the 4th quarter and in the most stressful situations possible.

Let's face it, in today's world we're not likely to be eaten by a T-Rex on our way to work or be playing in the NBA finals, but we will be faced with stressful situations on a daily basis. Whether it's physical or mental, our lives are filled with responsibilities, relationships, deadlines, demands, and frustrations. While we will have no control over many of the variables in our lives we must remember we have the ability to take charge of preparing ourselves, our actions, and our reactions. If we truly believe in ourselves and our abilities, then there's nothing we can't handle or accomplish.

Here are some common forms of stress we will encounter on a daily basis.

Distress—is the typical form of stress that we hear about when people say they're "stressed out." It means they're overwhelmed in some way. It could be involving work, relationships, responsibilities, etc.

Eustress—is actually good stress. It can be due to social engagements, being pregnant, engaged, getting a new job, being in love, competing in a sporting event, etc.

Relationship Stress—is the stress due to the relationships we have with family members, significant others, friends, and coworkers.

Work stress—is the stress involving work responsibilities, demands, deadlines, coworker relationships, etc.

These forms of stress can all be classified as different, and yet they're all similar. They all involve our own perception and what our reaction will be. In the ideal situation, we will be able to walk the fine line between managing our good stress and bad stress in order to accomplish more without becoming overwhelmed or "stressed out" where we shut down, accomplish less, and can encounter serious health problems.

While I truly believe over time we all have the ability to practice stress management and prevent most major health problems involved with stress, it's very important to know the risk factors involved for both ourselves and our loved ones.

Stress (distress) can cause an array of health problems including, high blood pressure, diabetes, obesity, headaches, asthma, gastrointestinal problems, depression, Alzheimer's, premature aging, and even death.

Here is a list of common warning signs that you may be stressed out and should perhaps seek out medical attention. Warning signs can be emotional, cognitive, physical, behavioral, or all of the above.

Emotional signs of stress can include irritability, moodiness, sense of loneliness, agitation, and depression. People can be short tempered, shut down, and ostracize themselves from the outside world, which will only make things worse.

Cognitive signs of stress include inability to concentrate, bad judgment, pessimistic attitude, constant worrying, and anxiety. People often lose confidence in themselves and worry about their true ability to live up to expectations.

Physical symptoms of stress can include nausea, chest pain, muscle tightness and pain, diarrhea or constipation, and frequent colds. Stress can cause your fascia (the Saran-wrap like substance around your muscles) to tighten which can cause tightness, pain, and muscle pulls. People will often feel the tightness in their upper back, lower back, and hamstrings.

Behavioral symptoms of stress include loss of appetite or emotional eating, nail biting, fidgeting, irregular sleep, compulsive procrastination, and the utilization of unhealthy habits like cigarettes or alcohol to deal with stress.

If you or someone you care for has several of these warning signs, it may be time to seek medical attention, but there are several things you can do to decrease the bad stress in your life and accomplish more while being a less stressed and happier individual. Here are 12 tips for decreasing the bad (distress) stress in your life.

1. Breathe

It sounds so simple, but many of us forget to breathe and truly appreciate our breath. Without your breath, there is no life. If you can dedicate two to three minutes in the morning and at night to sit in a quiet place and just focus on your breath, you will decrease your stress levels significantly. Slow breaths are ideal. Breathe deeply in through the nose and out through your mouth. Think to yourself, "in with the good energy; out with the bad."

2. Exercise

It doesn't have to be an hour-long session or cardio or strength training, but move your body. If you don't have time for a workout, then walk 15-30 minutes a day. It will clear your mind, get your endorphins and adrenaline flowing, and you'll be more productive because of it. Exercise is like natures Prozac. It will release your "feel-good hormones" and decrease your stress naturally.

3. Eat Healthy

Your body craves nutrients, so reward it with nutrient dense foods.

We are often so busy; we don't eat breakfast or forget to eat all together. This is a dangerous game to play because it often ends with binging on unhealthy food. This leaves us feeling a lack of energy, stressed out, and overwhelmed. If we want optimum performance in life and at work, then the body needs optimum fuel. Greens, whole grains, lean proteins, and healthy fats are ideal to keep you running on high energy and decrease your stress levels. (For additional nutrition tips, see Chapter 17.)

4. Drink Water

Keep yourself hydrated with pure water. Busy people are often looking to get another coffee or soda fix, but caffeine has been proven to increase your stress hormones, so minimize the caffeinated beverages and drink more water. It will help cleanse your system and you'll feel healthier and more productive in the long run.

5. Sleep

Make sure you get proper sleep at night. Your body needs recovery time. A lot of lawyers have high stress levels and this can often lead to insomnia. Going to sleep at the same time every night and spending two to three minutes focusing on your breath beforehand will make proper sleep a habit that will lower your stress levels and give you more energy. If you're stressed about work go to sleep early and get an early start in the morning. You'll be more productive in a rested state.

6. Accept Change

The world is an extremely diverse place with millions of different viewpoints and things going on at once. Many of these variables are beyond our control. Accept change and adversity as a necessary part of life and you'll be less affected by your constantly changing environment and you'll be less stressed and more likely to thrive in whatever environment the future holds for you.

7. Avoid Stimulants

Lawyers often look to relieve their stress by smoking or drinking alcohol. This will only mask the stresses in your life temporarily and in the long run your stress levels will only be *enhanced* by these unnecessary stimulants.

8. Listen to Music and Dance

If you allow yourself to get lost in some good music on a regular basis, your stress levels will lower significantly. When you listen to good music you allow yourself to escape and take a clearer look at whatever situation is causing you stress. If you'd like to take it to another level, listen to music and do some dancing.

Dance like you mean it. If you've ever seen a small child dance, it's obvious they don't care what anybody thinks, and therefore they're usually having the most fun. Dance like a kid again. This will take your mind and body to a better place.

9. Read

Get lost in a good book before bed or during your commute. This will enable you to relax a bit before or after your day. There's no point in thinking of work 24/7. Reading is a great distraction that will decrease your stress levels as well.

10. "I'm Rubber; You're Glue"

As children, most of us have heard the sayings "I'm rubber; you're glue. Whatever you say to me bounces off and sticks to you," or "Sticks and stones may break my bones, but words will never hurt me." Throughout your life, you will encounter certain people who give off negative energy and certain people who give off positive energy. Embrace the positive energy in your life and ignore the negative energy.

Most people who are constantly negative are acting this way because they themselves are stressed out, unhappy, jealous, or just have low self-esteem. Most people who are giving off positive energy are confident, successful, and happier less stressed individuals. It's also important to remember that this energy is contagious; if you maintain a positive attitude, it can actually rub off on negative individuals and even if it doesn't, that's okay because you're rubber and they're glue (wink!).

11. Live in the Now

Most stressful situations are a result of us dwelling about something unpleasant that has happened in the past or planning for something unpleasant to happen in the future. If we can live in the now, we can constantly move forward and use positive visualization to plan for the future instead of dwelling on or planning for the worst. Be prepared for anything but put the past in the past and keep moving forward while utilizing positive visualization for the future.

12. Stay Optimistic

Last but certainly not least, look at the bright side of things. No matter what the situation there are always different ways of

211

looking at things. For example, if you're extremely busy at work, be thankful for the challenge that lies ahead and the fact that you have a job and your health (rather than getting stressed out).

Throughout our work and personal lives, we will encounter thousands of different situations that will cause stress. I'd like to take a moment to talk about transitioning and utilizing stress to your advantage so that much of the Distress that's causing you health problems can be transformed into eustress and enable you to thrive and perform better in a stressful environment whether it's at work or in your personal life.

If we look at some of the most stressful moments in our lives, they are often followed by some of the best moments in our lives. Let's look at a few possible examples:

• Your first child

• Taking the Bar exam

• Starting your own business or a new job

• Your first love

All of these events are wonderful and stressful at the same time. It's our *perception* of these events that determines just how wonderful or stressful they will be. The best thing we can do when faced with a stressful situation is to realize that there are always positive aspects as well as negative aspects to any event. Why not focus on the positive?

Look at stressful events as opportunities to thrive. Remember stress enables us to accomplish more, to increase our intelligence, and grow stronger – both mentally and physically – if used correctly.

While there are a lot of exercises and different ways to look at

212

stress, I think the most powerful tool we have in our battle against stress (distress) is to live our lives with confidence and integrity. Integrity is when your feelings match your words, which in turn match your actions.

I think many of us go through life seeking the approval of others. This is normal (especially among our coworkers and loved ones), but it can also be a recipe for disaster. While it's nice to receive positive reinforcement for our work or behaviors it's important not to be dependent on it. This can cause extremely high levels of stress if and when those individuals don't give us the approval we seek. If we truly believe in ourselves, we will take pride in our work and behaviors, and not require the approval of others. Don't get me wrong, it can be helpful to take constructive criticism from those who are truly trying to help you, but that's no reason to stress out. It's most important to be honest with yourself and others.

Many of the most successful people throughout history had to battle through stress, adversity, and believe in themselves without the approval of others. Here are two examples to inspire you:

Marie Curie, one of the greatest scientists in history had to study in Warsaw's underground "floating universities" because she was unable to attend the men-only university of Warsaw. She went on to win two Nobel prizes.

Steve Jobs was given up for adoption and dropped out of college only to become one of the greatest minds the technology industry has ever seen.

We live in a "stressed-out" society where most people are distressed by the things that are beyond their control. Instead of succumbing to this paradigm, choose to take full advantage of the things that are within your control. We can take care of our bodies by eating right, exercising, remembering to breathe, and getting proper rest. We can take care of our minds by living life with integrity and believing in ourselves and our abilities, while surrounding ourselves with people who exude positive energy. We can also avoid dwelling on past failures and always utilize positive visualization for future successes.

May you always maximize the good stress, minimize the bad stress, be a positive light in your own life and the lives of others, and accomplish anything and everything you set your mind to . . . because you can!

When it comes to stress . . .

"Whatever you perceive to be exists and whatever you do not perceive to be does not exist." —George Berkley

About Jason Rodriguez

After receiving his undergraduate degree from the State University of New York at Stony Brook, Jason spent several years working in the financial services industry. While working as a banker, he encountered a great deal of stress and found himself breaking down mentally and physically. He began his own personal journey towards becoming a health and fitness expert for the benefit of his father, himself, and everyone around him.

Website: FitnessJourneysNYC.com
Facebook: facebook.com/FitnessJourneysNY
Twitter: @jasonFITnyc

Chapter 17
Finding Your Balance and Stress Management with Simple Nutrition and Self-Care Tips
by Mary E. Davis

Let's face it, we all have stress in our lives and the workplace is becoming more demanding for all of us.

Technology – a necessary evil! We are always "on" with our phones via texting, e-mails and, of course, social media. Instant response and gratification has become a requirement in our society, not only in our personal lives, but in the workplace as well. So how do we maintain peace of mind and balance with our busy lifestyles and careers? By keeping it as simple as possible!

Most of us overly complicate healthy eating - it's really not as hard as we make it. Proper nutrition plays a major role in helping to maintain our stress levels by consuming foods that energize us versus making us lethargic.

One of the major keys to this is to eat breakfast and be consistent. Just like your mother always said, "Breakfast is the most important meal of the day." Breakfast comes from the words "breaking the fast" after sleeping. Skipping breakfast can set you up for over-eating later in the day. A healthy breakfast will give you energy and set the stage for smart decisions all day long.

Breakfast should combine complex carbs, fiber and protein. Some simple healthy choices are oatmeal, grapefruit with yogurt or an egg or almond butter on whole wheat toast. You should jump start your metabolism by eating breakfast within a half- hour upon waking which will help start your day in a positive way!

Fuel Your Body Throughout the Day with Healthy Meals and Snacks

A great way to maintain balance is fueling your body every three to four hours with healthy meals and snacks. This can seem like a difficult task with our busy schedules, but easy grab and go snacks will make the difference. Portion control is a major factor with foods, but if you are fueling your body properly throughout the day, you will find it easier not to overeat in one sitting. Here are a few simple snack ideas:

- Fruits—banana, apple, grapefruit, strawberries, berries

- Nuts—almonds, pistachios, cashews

- Carrots and Hummus

- Peanut Butter and Celery

- Turkey Wrap

These foods are easily accessible (grab-and-go) and can be eaten in between meals to keep the metabolism fueled, which will help to perform better physically as well as mentally. Eating this way increases BMR (baseline metabolic rate—how fast your body burns calories), increases energy, and decreases appetite.

If you struggle with fueling your body and eating every three to four hours, try food logging. There are plenty of free fitness applications for this and it will also help you stay on track or you can just use a notebook for logging. Logging will make you more aware of what you are putting in your body. Again, keep it simple!

You may have the best of intentions, but until you log, you really can't hold yourself accountable and maintain portion-control.

Food logging also helps target areas that need improvement. For instance, you may not realize you are eating 1000 calories at lunch. Instead, you wonder why you are lethargic after lunch and are not able to effectively produce due to overeating in one sitting. Be aware of how you feel after you eat certain foods. You may feel energized or you may feel sluggish, certain foods will affect your performance and decision making. Whole foods (foods without additives, in their natural forms) as opposed to processed foods will help you function better and have more mental clarity. Write as you go and don't wait until the end of the day to log. Be consistent!

Another added bonus of food logging is that studies have shown that people who log lose twice as much weight than those who don't log. So if you are looking to lose or maintain your weight, this is a great tip to help keep you balanced.

Stress-Busting Foods: How They Work

Foods can help balance stress in several ways. Comfort foods, like a bowl of warm oatmeal, boost levels of serotonin, a calming brain chemical. Other foods can cut levels of cortisol and adrenaline, stress hormones that take a toll on the body over time. And a healthy diet can counter the impact of stress, by building up the immune system and lowering blood pressure. Here are some great stress-buster foods:

> **Complex Carbs**—All carbs trigger the brain to make more serotonin. For a steady supply of this feel-good chemical, it's best to eat complex carbs, which are digested more slowly. Good choices include whole-grain breakfast cereals, breads, and pastas, as well as old-fashioned oatmeal. Complex carbs

can also help you feel balanced by stabilizing blood sugar levels throughout the day.

Fatty Fish—To keep stress in check, make friends with fatty fish. Omega-3 fatty acids, found in fish such as salmon and tuna, can prevent surges in stress hormones and may help protect against heart disease, mood disorders like depression, and PMS.

Pistachios—Pistachios, as well as other nuts and seeds, are good sources of healthy fats. Eating a handful of pistachios, walnuts, or almonds every day may help lower your cholesterol, ease inflammation in your heart's arteries, make diabetes less likely, and help protect you against the effects of stress. Don't overdo it, though: nuts are rich in calories.

Avocados—One of the best ways to reduce high blood pressure is to get enough potassium -- and half an avocado has more potassium than a medium-sized banana. Guacamole, made from avocado, just might be a healthy alternative when stress has you craving a high-fat treat. Avocados are high in fat and calories, though, so keep your portion size in control.

Raw Veggies—Crunchy raw vegetables can help ease stress in a purely mechanical way. Munching celery or carrot sticks helps release a clenched jaw, and that can ward off tension.

De-Stress with Exercise and Movement

Besides changing your diet, one of the best stress-busting strategies is to start exercising. Aerobic exercise boosts oxygen circulation and spurs your body to make feel-good chemicals called endorphins. Aim for 30 minutes of aerobic exercise three to four times a week.

Keep it moving in the office! Our society has become very sedentary working at our desks on computers all day long. Take a few minutes and get up and stretch, do some forward bends which help alleviate stress and anxiety.

Walk around the office to keep the body moving which will help "rev" up the metabolism. Take the long way to the bathroom, use the stairs not the elevator, park further away. Get yourself a pedometer to track your steps, this is a great motivating tool:

10,000 steps a day burns 500 calories,
7 days per week is 3500 calories = 1 lb. weight loss per week

Drink Your Water!

Hydrating your body throughout the day is crucial in maintaining balance and reducing stress. If you're feeling drained and depleted, get a pick-me-up with water. Dehydration makes you feel tired and water boosts your energy. In addition, the right amount of water will help your heart pump your blood more effectively and also helps your blood transport oxygen and other essential nutrients to your cells.

Eat more fruits and vegetables since their high water content adds to your hydration. About 20 percent of our fluid intake comes from foods.

To keep stress levels down, keep a glass of water at your desk or carry a sports bottle and sip regularly. The goal is to drink at least 64 ounces (about two quarts) of water per day. If you forget to drink your water, set a reminder on your phone and this will help you in staying hydrated throughout the day. Always start your day with a glass of water to re-hydrate your body after a good night's sleep. When properly hydrated, you will not only feel better, you will be more efficient and productive.

Stress is something that will never go away completely but how we manage it is what counts. You have more control than you think and by simply nourishing your body with healthy foods and staying hydrated will help reduce your stress levels.

Practicing Self-Care is an Essential Part of Staying Balanced and Grounded

One of the main components of practicing self-care is feeding your body with healthy, nutritious foods. It's very easy to succumb to the fast food and sugar temptations in our society since they are everywhere. However part of self-care is to nourish your body with healthy and nutritious foods. Having a splurge once in a while is okay, but don't make this a habit – be sure you maintain a well-balanced diet.

Practicing self-care not only makes us feel better, it also helps us function at our best. It's during hectic and stressful times that we need to take care of ourselves by moving our bodies, getting enough sleep, not skipping meals, take a breather and preserve our boundaries. Here are seven essential self-care tips:

1. Massage Therapy has grown tremendously over the last few years because we have more stress than ever. We are constantly hunched over on our computers and phones and have more neck and back issues than ever in addition to poor posture. Massages have become a necessity for not only helping pain management but also to relieve everyday stress. Studies have shown that an hour massage is comparable to eight hours of relaxation. Be sure to get your massages!

2. Engage in self-care activities that you actually enjoy the most—read a book, watch a comedy, practice Yoga, have a spa treatment or take a walk. Whatever it is that you enjoy, make sure you are doing it. It's easy to get caught up in our busy lives, but it is important to take a step back and enjoy life too!

3. Find some quiet time and reflect. Busy does not necessarily mean happiness, we all need time to sit still and do a quick check-in physically, emotionally, spiritually and ask "What do I need?" or "What do I notice?"

4. Establish goals for yourself; be sure to carve out timeframes for your career and where you want to be in one year, five years, and ten years. This will help you stay on track and achieve your goals.

5. Ask for help. When your plate is too full or you are feeling overwhelmed, don't be afraid to ask for help. You'd be surprised as to who may help you.

6. Letting go of people that do not bring out the best in you is something we all need to do. Every once in a while, we have to "clean house" and sometimes we just outgrow people. It is truly important that we are all aware of the company we keep and how they affect our happiness and well-being. Just like we make healthy choices for the foods we put in our bodies, we must do the same with our friendships and relationships.

7. Practice Self-Forgiveness—don't beat yourself up, have no regrets and let go of the past. Freeing yourself of these things will help you live a happier, more peaceful life.

The goal is to "Keep it Simple" in these busy times and by incorporating these tips in your everyday life will ensure a healthier, more balanced mind and body in the workplace as well as in your personal life. The balanced approach is not a fad or a diet. It's a way of life that works, which consists of maintaining healthy eating habits as well as practicing self-care. Most of all consistency is key, so practicing these steps each day will automatically become your way of life!

About Mary E. Davis

Mary E. Davis is a graduate of the Institute of Integrative Nutrition (the world's largest nutrition school), a Certified Holistic Health and Nutrition Coach (Accredited through the American Association of Drugless Practitioners), and a Certified Yoga Instructor through Starseed Yoga and Healing in Montclair, NJ. She has over ten years experience in health and wellness and is passionate about helping others feel and look their best. Mary is part of the Esquire Coaching team.

Website: ZensTheWay.com

Chapter 18
Simple Strategies to Honor Yourself and Your Personal Relationships Amidst Your Demanding Career
by José Albino

Are the demands of your career causing time constraints that are affecting the quality of your life? Would your life be richer and less stressful if you were using your time more wisely to balance your relationships? The late great visionary William Penn, who inspired our Constitution and founded the state of Pennsylvania, stated, "Time is what we want most but what we use worst." This belief is easy to understand given the increasing demands of our daily work lives, particularly the pressures and responsibilities of those who practice law. Time, being a delicate yet powerful construct, can't be bought, bartered, or willed. As such it is understandable that simply thinking about how we utilize and prioritize our time can be paralyzing and overwhelming. To maximize the efficacy of what we do with our time, however, we can take strategic steps to manage its suspended energy and learn to master it in the context of our work-life balance.

The following narrative will offer you actionable and practical strategies and approaches that will help you manage both concerns of personal care and the strengthening of important personal relationships when career demands present competing time consuming priorities. Some of the key questions that will be answered here will be: how to manage and approach your personal care needs; how to get creative with spending time with a loved one when your work schedule is non-negotiable; and how to maximize quality time with a loved one.

Before moving forward, however, it's important to acknowledge that having a blue print of the amount of time and when you spend said time on work-related responsibilities is critical to the success of balancing your life on the heels of your career demands. I encourage you to take some time out and create a one-week time blueprint (including weekends) of the time that you are engaging in work-related activities, from the moment that you wake up in the morning to when you go to bed at night. This can include, for example, returning phone calls, reading e-mails, reviewing documents, and attending office or client meetings. If your schedule differs from week to week, it is acceptable to guesstimate. After doing this, you will be clearer on when you have disposable time available and you can begin mapping out how and when you are going to focus on honoring yourself and your relationships.

Honoring Yourself

Many lawyers, whether a sole proprietor, associate or partner in a firm, have excessive and intense demands that can create enmeshment with other non-work related priorities. Some of these demands may include fiscal concerns, internal reports, staffing concerns, chairing/attending meetings and the omnipresent insistent and time consuming client. This is not an easy web to untangle, but setting boundaries, and negotiating expectations, particularly with in the early stages of the relationship with clients, can undeniably reduce stress. The precursor to managing these problems, however, is managing the expectations of the relationship you have with yourself.

We are a culture that often neglects our own needs. This can be because of the disease to please, inability to say no, or simply not knowing how to create healthy restrictions on our time that will enable us to take care of our needs. It is not selfish, as sometimes we lead ourselves to believe. It is necessary as it creates the energetic space necessary to cultivate consciousness within ourselves and with those around us. Personal care is simply engaging in activities (typically during your spare time) that bring you joy and balance your mental and physical needs. To some this can also involve the spiritual. According to Clinical Psychologist Dr. Gionta, "self-care is a long-term lifestyle approach to how you live your life. It is something you do on a regular, consistent basis, and becomes an integral part of your life." She believes that a good self-care practice is a key component to effective stress management.

A critical element to understanding, and ultimately engaging in self-care strategies, is to honestly acknowledge what happens when you don't set expectations and boundaries with yourself with the goal of nurturing yourself. When your own health and well-being suffer it severely affects your stress levels. These stressors can manifest themselves in many ways such as weight gain/loss, sleeplessness, immune suppression, chronic fatigue, irritability and loss of enjoyment of activities you used to engage in, which can lead to depression and anxiety. Prolonged exposure to such symptoms can lead to serious medical problems, such as diabetes and heart disease, among others. A lack of self-care has serious implications. This in turn affects your presence in the family and other areas of your life, especially at work. This is particularly threatening for lawyers because your optimal availability is linked to career success. But you must acknowledge that you come first before anyone and anything. It's synonymous to the emergency protocol when flying - put on your mask before you help others with theirs. Focusing on your self-care, particularly in a demanding time-consuming career in law, is paramount.

Let's focus on what that looks like for you. Understand that there are no best practices in relation to self-care needs, only what is right for you. In order to engage in the necessary steps to begin taking care of yourself, ask yourself: on a scale of one to ten, with ten being the highest amount of care, - how do I rate myself when it comes to taking care of myself and my needs? Your answer points to the dimension of changes you need to make in your life to move you towards a ten. I offer you the following strategies and points of consideration when addressing your personal care.

List It

Lists are like money: not the most important thing in life, but when you have them, it makes life and your choices simpler. When you create lists, they trigger thoughts and emotions that facilitate concrete visuals of what you want to accomplish, tackle, or process. In order to jog your memory, start by asking yourself what activities feed your spirit and/or nurture your soul. What brings you joy that you are depriving yourself of? After this, create a list of the top five activities (or more) that energize and renew you. For some, self-care can mean an occasional walk, cooking, Yoga, meditation, exercising, catching up with friends or gardening. Whatever it is, write it down. Chances are, if it flows into your consciousness, it is important to you.

Schedule It

More and more studies suggest that engaging in frequent pleasurable activities and behaviors release health promoting natural "feel-good" chemicals produced by the brain known as endorphins. The more pleasurable activities you engage in, the better you will feel. Knowing this, I encourage you to plug in the frequency with which you plan to realistically engage on the identified activities throughout your weekly/monthly calendar. Routines give us stability and security. Ten minutes of meditation three times a week? Go to the gym two times a week? Approach these commitments with the same conviction and allegiance you approach work-related responsibilities. Remember that these are dates with yourself, the longest and most cherished relationship of your life, and therefore this time should be considered non-negotiable.

Expect Deviation

Chances are that if what has been referenced thus far resonates with you, you are at minimum, considering paying more attention to your personal care needs. I applaud that. But change needs to be approached with caution, particularly as it relates to new habits. Creating new habits for ourselves require a steely and disciplined resolve. Undoing old habits is probably more exhausting than creating new ones, but doable. It is critical to recognize that, while sometimes you may not reach all your self-care goals as desired, achieving one or a few a week or month is better than achieving none. When goals are not reached, simply make the decision to shift your thinking and recognize that you have the choice of starting again. Remind yourself that when you do focus on nurturing yourself, you will be more engaged and present with those around you. I offer you to repeat this simple mantra to yourself—"A better me. A better us."

Communicate It

A large part of why we dishonor the boundaries we create for ourselves is because we don't communicate them with the people that need to be aware of them. It's critical that the people you are in relationship with (client, spouse, boss, etc.) know the time slots during your day that you are tending to personal care needs and as such are not flexible. For example, if you block out 7-:00 p.m. to 8:30 p.m. Tuesdays and Thursdays to practice Yoga, then your partner should not interrupt that time. In addition, a demanding client may simply need to know that you have a "standing" occurrence during that time and as such, you are not reachable. Clear communication leads to respected expectations. While you should hold yourself accountable for your actions, you fiercely need to hold others accountable to honoring and respecting the boundaries you set for yourself as well.

Know Your Limits

Lawyers are undoubtedly driven, savvy and steadfast individuals that approach their work by a black and white legal doctrine. As such, those in the field recognize the importance and the parameters of possessing specialized education, skill sets, and expertise levels. Part of caring for yourself and your needs involves recognizing when you need to look outside of yourself and seek the assistance of a professional. If you need to, hire someone during this journey do so. For example, hiring a trained professional, such as a therapist or coach, can help you uncover the blocks that are contributing to possible chronic neglectful behaviors. Similarly, a nutritionist can help you develop a nutritional plan appropriate for your lifestyle. Instituting a mindset and practices that are going to make you a better you takes dedication, work and help from others as well.

Honoring Your Relationships

"Cherish your human connections - your relationships with friends and family." —Barbara Bush

It is a common belief that a majority of lawyers spend more waking hours physically at work and/or tending to their work responsibilities than they do at home or nurturing personal and intimate relationships. This belief can create a shift in the dynamics that in turn can be very difficult to re-stabilize with our family of choice or of origin. These are the top people in our lives that we are 100 percent committed to *investing* in, and as such, the limited amount of disposable time we have honoring them. This can include spouses, partners, mothers, in-laws, children, pastor, etc.

Existentialist Psychologist Rollo May stated that the reason for our existence is simply to love and be loved. And while love does have many forms, individuals want to feel like they matter, are being respected and appreciated in a relationship. But career demands, and technology, are creating darker blurred lines that don't allow us to strengthen our relationships to the extent that perhaps we would like. Furthermore, they don't help facilitate the time required to allow us to feel connected and present to the magnitude we would like with our loved ones.

The reality is that we have to work because of the financial security that our careers provide. There are mortgages, tuition and healthcare bills to consider. Similarly, there are relationships we have to nurture if we decide that they are going to continue and grow. However, we can't navigate our lives without either. The difficulty then is that both create competing urgencies because the demands of both are seen as priorities for the parties involved. If not managed creatively, stress can slowly rear its seemingly omnipresent head. How you navigate and set boundaries and expectations with your loved ones amidst your inflexible career demands, however, is a matter of, like self-care, having a strategy in place. And because a loved one is also genuinely invested in the relationship as well, their level of understanding of the parameters that need to be set for the sake of nurturing the relationship, and the reasons for them, are far less stressful than the plethora of demands that a career in law embodies.

Akin to time, personal relationships are extremely important and need to be approached with accountability, responsibility, effort and diligence. Like self-care, people who have good, solid relationships in their personal lives are more effective in their career. I encourage you to use the time blueprint referenced earlier to also schedule time with your loved ones. Here's what you can do to get the ball rolling on creating stronger relationships with those that are important in your life.

Initiate and Communicate

More often than not, if you are the one that works the long hours, your loved one is probably the one feeling neglected and unappreciated. Taking initiative evens the plateau and makes people feel heard and cherished. Ask the person when is the best time to sit down with them and explain that you acknowledge that there is work to be done in moving the relationship forward and you are ready to recommit and partner with them to take steps to do so.

People are helpers by nature and always want to be part of the solution. Enlist your loved one to help you come up with creative and realistic ways to strengthen the relationship within the context of your work and self-care need boundaries. Inviting them to be part of the solutions is validating that they too have a voice in the relationship.

Initiate a transparent conversation with your loved one and create a verbal agreement that recognizes and validates that, given the nature of your career, time constraints are and will be a factor in the relationship. Focus on the intention behind the conversation and the commitment it will take from both or all individuals involved to move the relationship forward. Everyone needs to have mutual buy-in in order for the strategies that will be implemented to be successful.

Quality Time

The traditional date night or visit to see your mother or best friend still operates with simplicity. Set a date, time and location and voila, you are good to go. Time together should be relaxed and organic. However, intentional connection and growth within any relationship requires work and dedication and because of this, some effort should be placed on planning on how to maximize some of the dates you spend together.

Engage in an activity that you both enjoy and alternate who picks the next activity, ensuring that you both begin to engage in each other's hobbies. This fosters a sense of inclusion and genuineness towards each other's interests and posits a sense of equivalence within the relationship.

Focus on activities where you are learning more about each other, (or persons) and deepen human connection. Going to the movies, for example, with your kid or partner does not lend for transformative and meaningful communication – the force behind an involved relationship - when time together is already a factor. Get creative and engage in dialogue where curiosity of each others' thoughts and emotions are central. Involve tools or word games that strengthen bonds if necessary.

Be purposefully inquisitive. If the ball is in your court in terms of needing to strengthen a particular relationship, you may need to bite the bullet in terms of making the time together not about you. Forfeit talking about yourself and your work. Instead, intentionally ask your loved ones appropriately probing questions about what is going in their life that genuinely makes them feel that you want to enter their world. Catch them up on life at another time.

Consider being two places at once, sort of. I had an extremely busy colleague who used to have her periodic brunch dates with her husband while their two age appropriate kids sat at a comfortable distance. After their much needed intimate time together, they would scoop up the kids at their table and head to family time together. You can exercise a similar strategy by maximizing your geography, having lunch with, say your sister and afterwards meet your best friend somewhere in the neighborhood for dessert.

Plug In

There is nothing better than one-on-one quality time, but if you have discussed and all parties involved have accepted the realities of a relationship that is going to have time constraints, video conferencing and chatting software such as Skype can help you engage in virtual quality time together. Creative ways to do this include scheduling a meal with your spouse during a lunch hour, helping your kids with their homework on the train ride home, sharing a glass of wine with your brother over the weekend, and coordinating face time with your frail mother via her home health aide. Along the same lines, you can use text messaging and e-mails to send mindful notes throughout the day or week to foster connection. This can be trivial, and amidst daily work life, one can get forgetful. Thankfully, you can register for automatic text and e-mail software and applications that allow you to pre-input messages and the dates and times you want them sent to your loved ones. You can exercise the same pre-arranged approach with companies that provide goods and merchandise so that you won't forget important dates, such as birthdays and anniversaries. A simple internet search can get you on the right path.

Implementing some of the strategies and approaches that are provided here that resonate with you, coupled with your ingenuity and discipline, will enable you to move toward a more streamlined lifestyle that has the capacity to improve your quality of life and deepen the relationship you have with yourself and your loved ones. Having a better grasp on how and when to manage and honor your career, your needs and your relationships is simply the beginning of your journey, not your destination.

About José Albino

José Albino is a Certified Life and Empowerment Coach, a trained psychotherapist, and consultant for Esquire Coaching. He fuses modalities and techniques from both disciplines to empower individuals to strengthen their courage and confidence in order to facilitate concrete and sustainable shifts in their lives. He received his B.A. in Psychology from the University at Albany, M.A. in Counseling from George Washington University and certifications from IPECand NYU School of Social Work.

Website: JoseAlbinoLifeCoach.com
LinkedIn: linkedin.com/in/josealbinolifecoach
Twitter: @JoseAlbinoCoach

Chapter 19
Cultivating Inner Peace
by Reverend Ketema Mason

Are you serious? Cultivate Inner Peace? What does that even mean? Regardless of what it is or what it means, I don't have time for it. I have deliberations in the morning, an arraignment in the afternoon, a briefing at the firm, and after that hopefully I have time to log this week's billable hours before my dinner plans. If I need Inner Peace, I'll have plenty of time for it while I'm sleeping. But come to think of it, I need to wake up early in the morning to meet with a client.

With all that said, there doesn't seem to be enough time to cultivate any peace, sleep, or otherwise. Nonetheless, my job is important to me, and this is what I need to do to excel at the firm. Conversely, it is also important to me that I have peace of mind so it all feels worth it. Okay, so if this cultivating inner peace thing is a way of achieving a healthy work-life balance, then I'm open to hear about. Please tell me more.

Before you explore the different ways to cultivate inner peace, it is important to first explain what inner peace is. *Inner peace* (or peace of mind) refers to the balance of peace between your mental, physical, and spiritual well-being. Being in a state of peace can give you an internal feeling of serenity and bliss that can serve as the healthy opposite to the stress and anxiety that you experience as an attorney. With inner peace, you will be able to act deliberately, rather than from a place of fear. You will have the ability to appreciate the present and not judge your past harshly. You will have feelings of connectedness that will give meaning to the work you do and prevent the feeling of burnout. Inner Peace can also be associated with terms such as bliss, happiness, enlightenment, nirvana, salaam, shalom, or conscious awareness. No matter what you refer to it as, cultivating your inner peace as an attorney can help you clarify your priorities, create healthy boundaries, and manage your time better.

The very nature of what you do as an attorney encompasses different levels of stress and anxiety. Your duties and responsibilities are both time consuming and intense. You are constantly on-call: reading e-mails all the time, responding to ongoing client demands, and you are being paid to worry about other people's problems. You are doing the best you can, to be the best you can in an ultra-competitive environment, all this while your peers, counterparts, and superiors are doing the same thing. Everyone is trying to be successful. Everyone is trying to become financially secure. Everyone is trying to take his or her career to the next level, whether it's winning an important case, making partner, or becoming a judge. Experiencing a high level of peace, joy, and happiness is what you need and deserve for the work you perform. You need to enjoy the fruits of your labor, you deserve to enjoy the different aspects of life, you need to have peace; your *Inner Peace*. By the end of this chapter, you'll feel as if you can live a more balanced and peaceful life overall.

"*Peace comes from within, do not seek it without.*"
—Buddha

Stress is unavoidable in any profession, particularly the legal profession. (See Chapter 16 for more information on good stress versus bad stress.) However, stress can be managed effectively. The ability to cultivate Inner Peace and have balance in your life is already with you, around you, or close to you. It is now a matter of recognizing what those things are and incorporating them into your daily life. In this chapter, you'll explore **twelve actionable items** that already exist to help bring forth your Inner Peace. Keep in mind that one size does not fit all, but trying some or all of the techniques may prove beneficial in achieving a healthy work-life balance.

> *"Journaling is writing the story of your life."*
> —Stacy Duplease

1. Journaling or Writing

Think about it: as an attorney you're already doing a great deal of writing for work. You are writing opening and closing arguments; you are drafting depositions, motions and appeals; you are revising contracts, and writing legal memos. The very nature of what you do for a living gives you the talent as a writer. Now imagine taking this skill and applying it to your personal life so that you can do therapeutic writing. *Therapeutic writing allows you to express your feelings to help ease the burden of what you may experience during the course of the day.* Picture yourself keeping a journal to highlight when you made partner, writing reflections from the courtroom, venting frustration about a negative client interaction, or a daily account of why you love being an attorney. With journaling, your writing talent now has a new form of personal expression. If journaling is not your thing, consider writing poetry, stories, songs, or simply a letter (or e-mail) to friends "just because." Choose whichever form works best for you. Journaling will give you a chance to use your writing talent to reduce stress, express gratitude, and enhance your creativity.

"You cannot always control what goes on outside but you can always control what goes on inside."
—Wayne Dyer

2. Meditating

There is a familiar comment a judge makes in the courtroom, "Let's take a 15 minute recess before we reconvene." This seems like a great opportunity for you to gather your thoughts and temper emotions. Did you know that this is a form of meditation? When you think of meditation, you probably think of someone doing Yoga, sitting in the lotus position with his or her legs crossed and palms up. So while this is partially true, meditation is the practice of training your mind to go into a mode of consciousness. There are many techniques (including Yoga) that are used to practice the act of meditation. Each one helps promote relaxation, sustain single-mindedness (focus), relieve anxiety, engender compassion, and build your internal energy. Some techniques include sitting in an active way, breathing, closing one's eyes, using prayer beads, journaling, or utilizing a mantra (repeated word or phrase). Here is an example of a counting mantra you can use as a meditative practice before your 15 minutes are up: "123, 234, 345, 456, 567, 678, etc." Your meditative practice doesn't have to be lengthy—a few minutes will suffice.

"Prayer is the Spirit speaking truth to truth."
—Philip James Bailey

3. Praying

As a lawyer, you're often in a position where you must be persuasive, asking others to believe in your truth. You are asking them to understand your position, and rendering a result that is favorable for you. Praying, in this sense, is no different. Praying is the act of seeking an active rapport or deliberate communication with God, a deity, the Divine, an Ancestor, a lofty idea, or your Truth. Prayer may be formal or informal. In a moment of prayer, you can use that dialogue to express gratitude, ask for guidance, regain focus, muster courage, or seek determination. Prayer beads, which are used by all major faiths and spiritual beliefs, can also be used to help focus your prayers and remind you to pray as you carry them.

"The first duty of love is to listen."
—Paul Tillich

4. Listening

As a lawyer, you have learned to carefully listen (e.g., instructions by the judge, causes of action in a client's story, opposing side's objectives in negotiations). All this conscious listening during the course of your day can be exhausting. You always keep a mindful ear so that you don't miss anything important! What if you let your mind be at ease and just listen for relaxation, enjoyment, or peace? Listening to music can bring about those feelings. Have you ever noticed the feeling you get when you listen to your favorite type of music? Whether it is country, rap, rock, reggae, pop or whatever you like, it can invoke various emotions needed to focus your attention or get you out of the funk you may be in. Listening to people singing, playing instruments, or the simple sounds of nature can also serve as easy listening opportunities to promote your inner calm.

"Variety is the spice of life."
—Common Cliché

5. Traveling

You have worked so hard, and now you are rewarding yourself with some time off. Is there a better way to regain your equilibrium than to go traveling somewhere other than home? Traveling provides you access to your inner peace by giving you the necessary time for solitude, reflection, relaxation and introspection. The ability to add traveling as an active part of your lifestyle gives you a variety of knowledge, experiences, visuals, and long-lasting memories that can deepen conversations with other people. Motives to traveling include pleasure, relaxation, discovery and exploration, getting to know other cultures, and taking personal time for building interpersonal relationships.

"When you know better you do better."
—Nikki Bailey

6. Researching

Neil Armstrong once said, "Research is creating opportunity." As an attorney, you are researching laws, regulations and precedents to create an opportunity for a favorable result for your client. That increased stock of knowledge is used to establish or confirm facts, reaffirm the results of previous work, solve new or existing problems, or develop and discover new ideas. There is also an opportunity to apply research knowledge to your well-being and personal growth. Research for the benefit of personal growth and well-being provides you with a new level of awareness, thought-provoking ideas, insightful opinions, and the understanding of a personally selected topic other than those in law. With an increase of personal research in the areas of the science, humanities, arts, economics, social science, business, and marketing, you may find you have hidden talents revealed, the mastery of a skill, or the ability to create your own law firm.

> *"In order to carry a positive action*
> *we must develop here a positive vision."*
> — Dalai Lama

7. Visioning or Projection

Visualizing a favorable outcome and thinking positively create success. Visioning is the process by which you decide what you want your future to look like. You want to be a rainmaker? Say it as a mantra. You want to make partner this year? Project that as a goal in your journal. You want to travel to the safari this summer? Visualize yourself in the safari hearing nature around you. Create a vision statement to provide a timeframe to implement and meet your personal expectations. A vision statement is a personally written outline declaring what you want to be, how you get there, and how long it will take. Similar to a corporate mission statement, your vision statement gives you a sense of direction, purpose, and intention towards your expectations. Keep your vision statement clear and concise, and no more than two to three sentences long so that you can you can edit, revise, or change it all together.

*"If you're respectful by habit, constantly honoring the worthy,
four things increase: long life, beauty, happiness, strength."*
—Buddha

8. Worshipping

As an attorney you follow a code of ethics, you uphold the law, and you honor the oath you took after passing the bar exam. You are acknowledging a higher legal authority for the purpose of being an attorney. Worship is a similar acknowledgement towards a higher authority for being spiritual. Evelyn Underhill (1946) defines worship as "the absolute acknowledgement of all that lies beyond us." That acknowledgement can be realized through religion, nature, history, science, art, or human life and character. Whichever honors your truth can give comfort and solace if you question your purpose. Keep in mind that worship is a personal expression of spiritually. There is no specific length of time needed to make it applicable. That time will vary depending on your preference and observation. That observation can occur in a place of worship, at an altar, in your home, or even by taking a moment of silence. An example of simple worship can be to honor this very moment in time by saying: "Thank for the gift known as the present!" (Note: The difference between prayer and worship is that prayer is the *inward* dialogue towards your spiritual truth, whereas worship is the *outward* expression to that same truth.

"I never met a chocolate I didn't like."
—Deanna Troi in Star Trek

246

9. Healthy Indulgence

Remember the feeling you had when your parents made your favorite meal because they didn't think you were 'Your usual happy self'? Remember how much better you felt once you finished that meal? You can recreate that positive feeling in your life today by having healthy indulgence of things you really enjoy, such as "Good Mood Food." If you want to attend a professional sporting event during the year, go for it! If you go shopping for a new suit every time you win a case, congratulations! If you are having a second slice of that chocolate pie because you have to work late, enjoy! Allowing yourself a healthy indulgence of the things you enjoy most provides instant stress relief for the occurrences that may disrupt your balance. Nevertheless, as the saying goes *"Everything in Moderation."* So keep your indulgence healthy, by utilizing it once a week, a month, a year, or in case of emergency. The risk of over-exposure to your healthy indulgence is that you may become used to it and then it doesn't have the intended effect of instant stress relief.

"Communication—the human connection—is the key to personal and career success."
—Paul J. Meyer

10. Communication

You are paying attention to the facial expressions and body language of your clients. You are conveying your position to the jury during opening arguments of a civil case. You sent the paralegal a message to conduct some beneficial legal research. This constant communication is the act by which one person gives or receives information from another person about that person's needs, desires, perceptions, or knowledge. As an attorney, when you are able to see the legal profession and community through communication, its daily ebbs and flows create a human connection. Herein lays the chance for you to have communication with like minds within an organization of other attorneys. There are many national legal organizations you can find through research that can provide you with publications, resources, and advocacy. Connecting with other attorneys that share your passion, doubts, and success, can give you an outlet to create inner peace and get back to your sense of purpose. You can also consider signing up for a prayer group, Yoga, meditation, or a number of other online groups surrounding your personal interests.

> *"Your breath can be the foundation of your inner peace."*
> —Ketema S. Mason

11. Breathing

You have heard the different iterations of the breath: "Breathe!" "Take a deep breath" or "Keep breathing." Breathing is the process that delivers oxygen to where it is needed in your body and removes carbon dioxide. Breathing is also a part of physiological respiration and is required to sustain life. It is one of the few bodily functions that, within limits, can be controlled consciously. Keeping this in mind, the conscious control of your breath can become a central place to foster your inner peace. In moments of anxiety, find your breath, notice your breath, and appreciate your breath. Psychologically, this type of breathing can act as a form of meditation. For example, breathe in an attitude of 'peace' and breathe out anxiety.

*"The art of being happy lies in the power of
extracting happiness from common things."*
—Henry Ward Beecher

12. Creating a Personal Sabbath

One of the earlier declarations in the *Ten Commandments* states
"Remember the Sabbath day, and to keep it holy." Generally
speaking, Sabbath is a weekly day for rest or time of worship.
Observed in the Abrahamic religions, it is a weekly observance of
different viewpoints and unique practices. With the religious
connotation aside, creating your own personal Sabbath is a way for
you to improve the weekly rhythm of your life and create spiritual
depth. You can choose a designated day of the week to keep a
journal, meditate, pray, sing, travel, research, visualize, worship,
make love, eat 'Good Mood Food' or simply rest. Creating your
own personal Sabbath will encourage you to unhook from the legal
treadmill you are on each week, recharge your own battery and let
you see that the work you do as an attorney provides a just and fair
society for us all.

Finding the Way to Your Inner Peace

You may have noticed while reading this chapter that many of the
recommendations seemed to coincide with each other. The
common thread among them all is you; your inner peace comes
from within. Start with the reality that you are a great attorney,
then feel good about yourself as a person, and understand the gifts
you already have to cultivate inner peace. Work at perfecting these
gifts so that becoming a "rainmaker" coalesces with helping
humanity. Understand there is another kind of peace that can be
achieved. The peace among human beings of all nationalities,
races, religions, and differing viewpoints lies in the fairness of due

process. In this regard, you are the gatekeeper of humanity's outer peace. The search for your inner peace and your calling as an attorney is your human connectedness with the world.

"Without first developing inner peace, outer peace is impossible."
—Ven. Geshe Kelsang Gyatso

About Ketema Mason

Rev. Ketema S. Mason is an Interfaith Minister from the One Spirit Interfaith Seminary (OSIS). Having completed his two years at OSIS, he has an active ministry at The Center of Spiritual Light® in New York City leading a Men's Group, monthly spiritual discussions, and training to become a Spiritual Life Coach. He earned his Master's degree from St. Joseph's College in Health Care Management in 2006.

Website: ReverendKMason.com
Facebook: facebook.com/kay.mason.5209
LinkedIn: linkedin.com/pub/ketema-s-mason/89/7a8/a9
Twitter: @RevKetema

Chapter 20
Raising the Bar:
Increasing Your Energy Levels
for Happiness & Success
by Nilda Carrasquillo

"The energy of the mind is the essence of life."
—Aristotle

In his book, *Energy Leadership: Transforming Your Workplace and Your Life from the Core*, Bruce D. Schneider writes, "Energy is one word that I have seen that differentiates great leaders from average leaders. Great leaders not only have positive energy, they contagiously spread this positive energy to others."

Energy is the power, strength and vigor required for sustained physical or mental activity. Your thoughts and your emotions drive your energy; your energy influences your level of performance. Schneider also introduces the seven levels of energy, which are described below.

Level 1—Victim

This level has the lowest amount of available strength and vigor, with the highest level of catabolic (negative) energy. When you are in Level 1, you are drained and lack motivation. You feel lethargic and take no action because you see your circumstances from a powerless victim's perspective.

Level 2—Conflict

This level has a little more strength then Level 1, but it is still negative. You are motivated by anger. You feel dissatisfaction and are willing to take some action that is provoked by anger or in reaction to anger (e.g., defiance).

Level 3—Responsibility

This is when you begin to build strength and vigor and have shifted into anabolic (positive) energy because you're accepting a greater deal of responsibility for your thoughts, actions, and emotions. You are solution-oriented, more forgiving and able to take action.

Level 4—Concern

At this level, you begin to start focusing on others and are supportive. You are team-oriented, compassionate and your action is motivated by being of service.

Level 5—Reconciliation

At this level, you release much of the judgment associated with the previous levels because you are able to reconcile differences and accept your circumstances. You experience greater control over your actions and reactions, and have greater inner peace because you see things as presenting opportunities: you feel more powerful, confident, courageous, and connected to others.

Level 6—Synthesis

At this level, there is high level of available strength and vigor because you are able to access more of your intuition and creative genius. This is the level that great leaders tap into to produce innovation. Here, you are proactive, visionary, and focused on the experience. You are calm and content.

Level 7—Nonjudgment

This is the highest level of available energy (and power). At this level, you are without judgment, experiencing absolute passion. You create, observe and experience simultaneously. A person at this level has mastered all previous levels and uses those experiences to enhance objectivity and nonjudgment.

It is important to acknowledge that energy fluctuates. You may experience different energy levels within the same day or over a period of time. Energy is like the waves: sometimes the tides are low; other times they are high. Either way, the ocean comes together and always continues to exist and have profound impact. The objective is to stay with high tides and swim with and not against the waves, recognizing there are natural periods of lows.

Even though energy fluctuates, from which energy level(s) do you tend to predominantly operate? How is your energy influencing your work, your life and your environment? To help you answer these questions, it is important to understand how thoughts and emotions affect your energy.

The Mind: Your Thoughts, Beliefs and Emotions

Your mind guides your thoughts and emotions. The thoughts are embedded in your core, deep within, and are influenced by your beliefs about yourself, others and life. Your core thoughts are primarily driven by messages that have been instilled in you as early as childhood, and have formed who you are. These messages have created your perception of yourself, others and the world. They have molded your behaviors and how you act and react. The great thing is that you can change your core thoughts. Thoughts are constructed by perceptions and self-awareness. For that reason, you have the power to alter how you perceive who you are, your circumstances and how you respond.

When thoughts and emotions are negative, they paralyze you and prevent you being clear or taking action. These thoughts may lead to feelings of hopelessness, apprehension, judgment and/or disbelief in self and/or others. When you think back to Levels 1 and 2, your energy is negative; you are at a place that does not serve you. There is not much fuel to keep you moving forward toward optimal happiness and success.

On the other hand, when you are in a positive state of mind, you are clear and in action with joy and satisfaction. You are in Levels 3 to 7, utilizing positive energy. You are more focused and put value on work and life, creating balance and success. Your thoughts may lead to feelings of are excitement, trust and hopefulness; you are focused and in constant action. You are driven and inspired by the alignment of your purpose, desire and intentions.

Our goal in life should be to have positive energy moving us from our core, inspiring our being, and our true self. Self-awareness is significant in this process. Once you are aware of your thoughts, then you can change them.

How to Determine and Shift Your Energy Level

The first step to increasing your energy level is to *increase your level of self-awareness*. Specifically, it is important to identify your core thoughts and any preconceived messages you may have received from others. To help you identify these thoughts and messages, engage in the following exercise: set aside time and find a quiet place where you can sit for at least 15 minutes (preferably longer). Focus on your breath. As you breathe in and out, relax. Allow yourself open up to what is going on within you. Think about a current work challenge you are facing. Pay attention to your thoughts and emotions. What is your level of energy? Observe whether you have messages that indicate how you "should" respond to the situation. What are the messages saying? How do they affect your thoughts and feelings? How are these thoughts holding you down or moving you forward? How can you give power to those messages that give you strength and vitality, while minimizing those that drain you? Write down your insights.

Now that you have shed light on your core thoughts, you can begin to change those that don't serve you. To effectively re-energize and raise your energy level, you must shift each of your energy-depleting thoughts. When you change your thoughts, you change your feelings and ultimately your behavior. For example, let's assume your challenge is a difficult client. If your core thought is, "I can't stand this client, but I really can't afford to lose him," you are likely to be at Levels 1 or 2. This thought will produce feelings of disdain or resentment, which in turn, will produce lethargic or apathetic behaviors (e.g., procrastinating on this client matter). Instead, imagine redirecting your thought to, "Although this client is difficult at times, I choose to focus on what I can control . . . providing excellent legal representation." This simple redirection of thoughts allows positive energy to flow, physically, mentally and emotionally.

By recognizing the level of energy you bring to each circumstance (personally and professionally), you are able to focus and direct your energy toward positive results. Keep in mind, success is driven by positive energy. When you are self-aware and clear, you are able to choose how to perceive your circumstances and how you react to stressors.

The next step to increasing your energy level is to *identify and manage stressors*. Stress is inevitable, however you need to manage stress, not avoid it or fight it, to keep a high positive level of energy. (See Chapter 16 for more information on stress.) When you avoid or fight stress, you are operating from a place of self-pity and/or anger (negative energy Levels 1 and 2). Negative or excessive stress consumes you spiritually, physically and mentally, affecting your ability to move forward in your practice, relationships and life. Remove this stress by changing your thoughts to something more positive as outlined above (note, it should be believable to you, not something pie-in-the-sky). For example, we have heard the cliché, "It's easier said than done." How about changing this thought to, "It is done easier than we think"? Wouldn't that make a big difference?

Managing stress involves owning and honing your power and taking responsibility. You'll need to operate from at least Levels 3, 4, or 5, by choosing to focus on solutions, act with compassion, and let go of judgment. Hold on to your new more positive thought and continue building on it. Positive thoughts generate positive feelings and emotions and move you forward with greater ease and satisfaction.

You can also manage stressors by connecting to your purpose and vision. Johnnie Cochran once said, "An opening statement is like a guide or a road map. It's a very delicate thing." This quote is perfect to better understand the power of setting an intention for success. Like with any journey, you have to know where you going and then use a map to guide you. As you build your practice, create your map, starting with a clear intention. Be clear about your ultimate goals, why they are important to you, and what actions you'll need to take to get there. An example is, "I will have X amount of clients by this date." Similar to the car that takes you on your road trip, you have to fuel yourself, physically, mentally and spiritually with positive energy. Stay present in the moment so you are not swayed by past worries, fear of the future, or fear of the unknown. Include in your map affirmations to help you hold on to the feelings of excitement, peace and confidence that your purpose or vision inspire.

Stressors can also be managed by recalling a time in your life where you overcame a difficulty. Think about a specific difficult situation or stressor you overcame. What thoughts and emotions come up for you when you reflect on that situation? Allow those positive thoughts and emotions to help you reduce your stress and negativity, and instill confidence that you can handle your current stressor. Take time to celebrate and embrace these important accomplishments.

Another important element in managing and reducing stress is self-care; get adequate rest, sleep and nutrients. (See Chapter 17 for more self-care tips.) Caring for the body, mind and soul makes it possible for you to maintain higher levels of positive energy. The higher your positive energy, the more connected you are to your intuition and the more open you are to seeing the opportunities in all areas of your life (Levels 5 and 6).

An additional step to increasing your energy level is to balance work/career and life.

In *"Cases and Chaos: Work-Life Balance Strategies for Busy Lawyers,"* Jatrine Bentsi-Enchill, J.D. CPCC, wrote that at the heart of successful work-life balance is both accomplishment and enjoyment. She stated it this way: "Accomplishment: getting the stuff we need to get done accomplished, and Enjoyment: having the time for loved ones, fun, rest, exercise and hobbies."

Work–life balance requires prioritizing between your work (career) and life (health, relationships, fun/joy and spirituality). The tendency is to focus on putting our energy toward managing our time. We make sure to pencil in our briefings, clients and other appointments. Yet, we are not intentional about how and when we are going to spend time with family and friends, much less with ourselves. (See Chapter 18 for more information on maintaining personal relationships.) We are constantly juggling at a fast past in the pursuit of accomplishing ultimate success. Nonetheless, we find we are perpetually exhausted, discontent and disconnected. We cannot minimize the value of time management. Effective time management can help shift energy. However, the goal is to see your life in its totality and ensure that each area of your life is getting the appropriate amount of attention it needs to thrive.

To move you forward in creating a "Happy Law Practice," focus on how you balance your mental, spiritual and physical energy. How are you balancing these areas of your life? Notice, are you surrounded by negative or positive energy? Is your mental, spiritual and physical energy supported by positive and constructive thoughts, emotions and actions? Important questions! Think about it: you put premium gas in your car, use the best batteries for your equipment and make sure you charge your cell phone and other electronics to keep you and your business moving. Yet, how do you fuel yourself and your key relationships? This type of fueling guarantees that you'll have the positive energy to move forward to create a happy and successful practice.

Who and what are you impacting, profoundly and positively, in your life and career? To have profound impact, you need to maintain a balance that will energize and propel your *whole (i.e., your physical, mental and spiritual)* self.

Clear Your Energetic Systems

So far, you have been presented the opportunity to understand how your life and career are affected by positive and negative energy. You have reflected on your own energy levels and the thoughts that create them. You've also discovered ways to manage those that do not serve you. The flow of positive energy is blocked by internal and external sources. To let the energy flow, you need to de-clutter. De-cluttering is a way to clear your energy systems, removing the blocks that hold you down. When you are mindful, you are able to recognize what is working for you and what is not.

Self-awareness opens you up to the opportunity to better understand the things that block your positive energy, so that you can energetically stand in your own power. The process of de-cluttering allows you to remove blocks to your positive energy.

Remove the Blockers from the Mind, Thoughts, and the Emotions

Let go of *being judgmental*. Although as a lawyer, you have to exercise discernment, this is not the same as being judgmental. Notice where you may be judging yourself or others and try to exercise compassion instead. This allows you to open up to self-love and acceptance. Energy attracts like energy; thus, as you release judgment, you will attract more people who will reciprocate.

Let go of *past negative experiences that weigh you down*. This requires you to make a conscious choice to accept the past and remove the emotional charge you have (e.g., through forgiveness, therapy, prayer, etc.). Only then are you able to embrace the moment and recognize opportunities.

Let go of *the need to always be in control*. There are times as a lawyer when you have to exercise control or oversight, but are you taking it too far? If so, learn to trust others and even your higher power. Ironically, you will gain, not lose power and build on positive, not negative energy.

Let go of the *uneasiness of illness, hostility or pain*. Instead put your focus on gratitude, which increases your positive energy.

Let go of *fear*. Is your fear paralyzing you from moving forward and taking action? If so, remind yourself of your many challenges and successes. Savor the positive thoughts and emotions and use it to fuel your positive energy.

Let go of *anger*. Anger usually represents that something needs to change in order to better honor you and/or your values. Find out what needs to change and take appropriate action. As you lift the anger, it opens you up to greater clarity, energizing you to create and take better actions overall.

Remove the blockers from your environment—space and relationships

In addition to de-cluttering your mind, you can de-clutter external things. When you de-clutter externally, pay close attention to your environment, your space, and your professional, personal and intimate relationships. You want to remove anything that does not serve you and stops you from moving forward energetically. You must intentionally work on yourself so you can breakdown your negative energy and have happiness, clarity, and abundance in all areas of your life.

Remove all the extra "stuff" that consumes your space – in your office, home, and even your car. This can include removing yourself from a space that brings your energy level down. Your external space is a reflection of what is going on internally. Freeing of space allows for more positive energy to flow. Freeing up space in your environment frees up space in your mind and soul.

Remove those people that keep themselves and you in a negative state, lethargic and/or angry, or have victim energy ("poor me"). As a preliminary matter, know what your values are and measure your relationships against them. This can be difficult for many reasons. For example, it may be a partner in your practice who is negative. You may not want to stop working with him/her because there is some value to the relationship. If there is value, then figure out how to change your circumstances and/or reaction so as to minimize reduced energy or happiness. You are the only person that you can change. Even when the negative person is your parent, sibling or child, remember you have options. Removing your loved ones from your space does not mean that you stop loving them; it means you love them and yourself enough to make healthy choices.

Remove all the things that do not serve you. Remove what weighs you down and holds you back. It's not selfishness; it's about being authentic and committed to your happiness and success. If you are hoarding or holding on to something that doesn't serve you, ask yourself: "What do I fear? What past thoughts or emotions am I holding on to?"

In summary, to raise the bar for ultimate happiness and success, dare to transform and increase your energy level. Envision who you want to be and choose to be authentic. By authentic, I mean the person that is confident and fueled by excitement and happiness from the core. Happiness from the core guarantees all around success. If you are not in your element, change your thoughts and behaviors. Create the authentic (and ideal) you. Keep it all together by maximizing on your positive energy. Make your happiness a priority. Reprioritize your values and think differently when necessary. Engage in self-care and gain deeper awareness. Spend time with people that exude positive energy.

Have a heart of gratitude and focus your energy on positive outcomes. Be honest with yourself, forgive yourself and believe in yourself. Live in the present. Shape and strengthen the leader that you aspire to be, and build a happy, energetic and successful law practice.

About Nilda Carrasquillo

Nilda M. Carrasquillo is a leadership, wellness and work-life balance coach and facilitator and Reiki practitioner. For over 20 years, she has worked with individuals challenged with drug addiction and life and social ills, helping them find their inner strength, get motivated and take action to make the change to a healthier and successful life. Nilda is part of the Esquire Coaching team.

Website: TeeCoaching.com
Facebook: facebook.com/TEECoaching
Twitter: @TEECoaching

Chapter 21
Success with Authenticity, Integrity & Heart
by Sandra Olper

Success can be defined in many ways. One definition is: "The achievement of something desired, planned or attempted." If we remove the word "desire" from that definition, the heart is left out. When we don't connect our achievements to our heart or when we don't have a clear idea of why it is important for us to achieve something, our success story is an empty one. When we take the time to connect our core values to the choices that we make and the person we want to be, then we have full integrity with ourselves. I don't know of a more rewarding success story than this.

Focus for a moment on this thought: "Everything must get done today! Now! You are already late!" Feel for a moment what it is like to go every day with "the mask" of one who must perform to the best of his/her ability, putting all the energy into that mask rather than coming from a place of authenticity. Feel what it is like to have every day be a race for more: more money, more clients, more "success," and needing to do things more efficiently! Are you feeling the pressure? How well can you breathe from here? Just writing about it makes me feel so tight, that I am now desperate to take a breath. So... go ahead, take a breath; it takes two seconds, and it allows you to shift gears and free yourself from how things are "supposed to be."

We live in a culture that has bought into the slogan of 'more is better'. Success means having a lot of money. Success means having many cars and materialistic things. Success means looking like a certain kind of beautiful. We are living such a fast-paced life that we tend to take these values and expectations from the outside and make them ours without questioning if we align with them or not. I am here to tell you to *pause*!

Now, imagine going to your firm every day feeling like you have a purpose, like you can access all of who you are, knowing that every fiber of your being can contribute to a greater success at work. Consider lawyers who are singers or musicians; or others who may be great soccer players or who love to ski. What if these lawyers could tap into the values behind these passions applying their creativity, their freedom, their sense of adventure, their humorous side or their intent to collaborate? This could lead to inspiration, teamwork and a more vibrant workplace. Imagine approaching that contract or that trial as if it was the Super Bowl, or a concert at Madison Square Garden? If you could show up at work with "all of you," wouldn't it feel more like PLAY? So, how do you feel now? Do you feel like there is more space to breathe?

I don't know what success means to you. Everybody on this planet is unique and he/she will define it differently. When you give yourself the gift of pausing, you receive the opportunity to re-examine what it is YOU want rather than what you have allowed society and your culture to dictate to you. Do you approach your work with your own core values or do you "disappear" behind your mask? If you have to leave most of who you are behind in order to be "successful," is it worth it? When you realize what it is you want and get clear about why it's important to you, then life becomes purposeful.

It's not enough to know your own core values. It takes a disciplined mind not to be tempted to go with the flow of what society says is "best" for you. Going against the current and learning to filter out the messages from society that don't mesh with your own values is of utmost importance to living an authentic life. Especially toxic are the messages that "more is better" and "you don't have enough." Lynn Twist, author of *The Soul of Money*, explains that we rarely experience that place of fulfillment because we are always chasing something else and wanting what we don't have. We rarely stop and appreciate and enjoy what is right in front of us. When you stop to appreciate what you have, a feeling of gratitude envelops you. Feeling gratitude is enriching because it reminds you of what's important.

The first step in being grateful is to notice and become aware of your surroundings. It is not a passive noticing; it is a noticing with intention. You can take a deep breath while commuting to work and really capture the beauty of a tree or the sky. This simple shift in your attention can change your whole day. You can look into somebody's eyes and acknowledge his or her humanity. We are usually so concerned with our 'to do' list that we miss all of these opportunities to connect with ourselves and feel joy.

When we fail to acknowledge the greatness that life has to offer, we hinder our daily interactions; we become robotic and it can tempt us to jump on the treadmill of the fast-paced life to emptiness. Learning to appreciate the little things in life opens doors for us. We often think, "When this _____ (big thing) happens to me, then I will be happy or successful or _____." But in practice, if you pay attention to the little everyday things and appreciate them, your heart will warm up, and you will become more open, accepting, patient and present, which will benefit your life and your practice. Isn't that worth a minute of your time here and there?

You may be making promises to yourself: "After this case or this client, I will be home and I will be more available to my friends and family." You may even be hoping to take better care of yourself physically by going to the gym or eating a healthy meal. When these promises go unfulfilled what you feel is frustration and self-loathing.

When you take care of yourself, it opens up doors for you to take care of your clients in the same manner. When you pause to become aware of what inspires you and what it is you want, you have the recipe to fill up your own "gas tank." This, in turn, will be beneficial to your firm and your clients since you will feel energized, purposeful, and you will also be more efficient. It can even be contagious.

The only person that can decide what quality of life you lead is you. You may not be able to change the world around you, but you can change how you experience it. One of my all-time favorite concepts is "Be, Do, Have." Who you are *being*, drives what you are *doing,* which in turn creates the results you are *having.* You have a choice every single day to *Be* the person you want to be. That doesn't mean things will always go right. It just means you will have the opportunity to learn from this experience and practice resilience. My message to you is not to quit your job to be happy, but rather, to take a moment to see the bigger picture, connect with what you value, and really reframe your perspective at work and your personal life. When you look through the lens of gratitude and appreciation rather than fear and survival, you change your whole experience.

In her book, *Living with Joy,* Sanaya Roman describes how gratitude is magnetic. If you are feeling like your work life is stagnant and constraining, one solution can be to pause and reflect on what it is that you enjoy about what you are working on rather than focusing on what you are worried about or on what you haven't yet finished. Once you find that positive quality, keep focusing on that aspect. This will enrich your overall feeling and it will have a ripple effect on your clients and co-workers. Appreciation can have a huge positive impact on your success at work. And when you appreciate the work of others around you, it feels good and serves as a motivator to keep going further. If acknowledging each other or appreciating each other's work is not the norm in your firm, bring that practice in, knowing it can do no harm and will most certainly increase fulfillment and productivity!

There are many jokes about lawyers being unethical or just being interested in the money and winning. One example of this is a cartoon that depicts two lawyers at a desk discussing strategy. One lawyer says to the other, "Is it right? Is it fair?" And the other responds, "Get a grip, Carlton-we're a law firm!" What if you could prove these stereotypes wrong? A culture of appreciation and gratitude is one way to combat this stereotype. Another way is by becoming more person-centered rather than problem-centered. Lawyers serve their clients not only as their attorneys but also as their teachers, their sounding boards, mediators, and protectors. As a lawyer, when you allow yourself to empathize with your clients, rather than be focused just on the facts, it allows the humanity and meaning of your work to shine through. You remain anchored in knowing that you are in service of another human being and what you are doing matters.

In order to retain a healthy perspective that what you do matters, it is important to actively work at living a balanced life. You are in a profession that can be highly demanding of your time and resources and can be quite results-based. Perfection is an illusion. You will never get there. It is another mask. Some of you may be parents; some of you may be taking care of an aging relative. When you set clear time boundaries between your work and family, you ensure that your whole being is fully realized. To be successful, your life needs to remain in balance. Natural laws are a perfect example of this. No matter what is going on, the day doesn't tell the night: "Hey, wait a little bit, I am not done yet."

If we think about the scales of justice, lawyers must seek balance between truth and fairness. The way to achieve this is through collecting evidence that supports either side. What if we were to put your personal life on one side of the scale and your work life on the other? What would it look like? Does it look the way you want it to look? How would the scales look if you stopped feeding the 'performance mask' and instead nurtured your most authentic and heart-felt self?

Let yourself write a new definition of success. Put your energy towards what matters most for you. Be aware of when you are wearing a mask. Make the conscious choice to take off your mask in service of living authentically. Be resilient against the voices around you that say 'more is better' and that 'there is not enough'. Be present and notice what is in front of you right now. Be committed to living a life of gratitude and appreciation. Take precious care of yourself so that you can take care of others, and when you find yourself overwhelmed, pause and remember that it is all in the perspective that you choose to hold. As you search for a more productive perspective, decide that you are going to pay attention to what is working rather than what is not. Really see the person in front of you. Stop and assess if things are balanced. "The key to keeping your balance is knowing when you've lost it" (lifelovequotesandsayings.com). Only you can make a difference in your life. You can change the way the scales tip, starting today. Begin gathering evidence for whatever it is you are seeking and make the scales tip in your favor. There is definitely justice for self-sustainability. Go find it and enjoy the journey!

About Sandra Olper

Sandra has a deep passion and amazing skill for helping others discover and become who they really want to be. As a coach, she encourages her clients to explore their values and make choices that will enable them to reach their full potential. Sandra received her B.A. in Psychology from Brandeis University. She specialized in Clinical Psychology from the UNAM (Mexico City). She is a graduate of CTI coaching and leadership certification programs.

Website: AtrioLifeCoaches.com
Facebook: facebook.com/sandra.olper
LinkedIn: linkedin.com/pub/sandra-olper/14/203/b0

Ready to Take it to the Next Level?

Thank you for reading *The Happy Law Practice: Expert Strategies to Build Business While Maintaining Peace of Mind.* We hope that you enjoyed the tips and strategies shared by our expert authors. Want more support in growing your book of business, expanding your leadership capabilities, or achieving greater work-life balance?

WE CAN HELP YOU TAKE YOUR CAREER TO THE NEXT LEVEL!

Esquire Coaching a national coaching and consulting firm dedicated to assisting lawyers be the best in their field without sacrificing their personal life. We can help address the specific needs of you and/or your firm, such as business development, strategic planning, leadership development, image consulting, and more. In addition to providing private individual coaching, Esquire Coaching also offers two signature programs that can help you develop essential skills to have a successful and balanced career:

ESQUIRE BUSINESS PROGRAM: Designed for the sole proprietor or small firm partner, this intensive 3-month crash-course will teach you the essentials to building a profitable business. You'll walk away with a concrete marketing action plan and system that will help you execute your plan.

ESQUIRE BALANCE PROGRAM: This program will help you achieve better work-life balance and peace of mind. By taking a comprehensive approach to your wellbeing, you'll reduce stress, create healthy boundaries, and manage your time better.

Ready to Take it to the Next Level?

Why take your career to the next level all by yourself when you can have a TEAM support you and give you the short cut to achieving your professional and personal goals?

We will provide you with a NO-OBLIGATION, FREE 2.0 STRATEGY SESSION

In this session, we will:

• **Determine what personal and professional goals will help you uplevel to the 2.0 version of you**

• **Find out the obstacles and consistent habits that will keep you operating at 1.0**

• **Recommend strategies to overcome those obstacles and propel you to 2.0**

So, are you ready to take it to the next level?
The first step is to contact us:

info@EsquireCoaching.com
800-871-9012, Ext.776250#
EsquireCoaching.com

"At the end of the day, let there be no excuses, no explanations, no regrets." —Steve Maraboli

ESQUIRE COACHING

Leading Attorneys to Extraordinary Personal & Professional Success